Alicia)
Keep your
Burning!
Cl—

IGNITE THE
SECRET

IGNITE THE
SECRET

19 Lessons for Business and Life

CHARLES HORTON

with contributions from
DAVE ALBIN & JOE WHITE

BROWN BOOKS
PUBLISHING GROUP

Ignite the Secret
19 Lessons for Business and Life

Brown Books Publishing Group
16250 Knoll Trail Drive, Suite 205
Dallas, Texas 75248
www.BrownBooks.com
(972) 381-0009

A New Era in Publishing®

ISBN 978-1-61254-875-3
Library of Congress Control Number 2016931113

Printed in the United States
10 9 8 7 6 5 4 3 2 1

For more information or to contact the author, please go to www.IgniteTheSecret.com.

Contents

A real decision is measured by the fact that you've taken new action.

—Tony Robbins, motivational speaker

Disclaimer: The activities described in this book are intended to be performed under professional supervision only. Do not try them at home without the proper training.

"If I Can Firewalk, What Else Can I Do?"

Stop. Wipe your feet. Celebrate.

I had done it. I had walked on fire, my bare feet touching a bed of coals. My body knew it—there was a tingling starting up from my soles, more an energized sensation than the burn I'd been expecting. But my mind was asking, *What just happened? How did I do that?*

I didn't know it then, but my life had just shifted to a whole new level. That firewalk lifted my consciousness in a way I didn't know was possible. It shook up my nervous system and released something in me that made me ask, *Hmmm, well, if I can firewalk, what else can I do?*

We all face the "fire" at times throughout our life—in business, in relationships, in our personal development. As a tool for everything from personal insight to professional success, the firewalk is unlike anything I've ever seen—one of the most unique things anybody can do if they want to change something in their life.

The nineteen lessons of this book come directly from Charles Horton's life experiences from three different companies, including his motivational business and the Firewalking Institute of Research and Education. Charles is a one-of-a-kind guy, a man of great honor and integrity who has an amazing story to tell—a lifelong entrepreneur, he came to firewalking as a convert like me—and as with the firewalking experience, I can't think of anyone who would fail to benefit from it. It's a story of personal development and professional success despite (or perhaps because of) many challenges and much difficulty. It's a story full of insight and wisdom that just about anyone—including you—can apply in their own career and life.

Now, you may be thinking, *How can Charles Horton's story help me? I'm the last person who would ever walk through fire.* Well, whether or not you ever choose to do a firewalk, these nineteen lessons can transform your life as if you had. And believe me, I certainly understand where you're coming from: I once felt quite sure *I* was the last person who would ever walk through fire—and it ended up transforming my life.

*****

One of my best friends had invited me to hear motivational speaker and self-help coach Tony Robbins at a four-day live event. He told me he'd get the tickets, and by the way, we'd be doing a firewalk.

As soon as those words came out of his mouth, fear shot through me like nothing I'd felt before. I had joined Alcoholics Anonymous seven years previously out of desperation. I was no stranger to fear, especially when it came to facing my demons. My recovery had included plenty of them—and insomnia had been one. In fact, I'd been up late one night and seen a Tony Robbins infomercial, so I'd ordered his thirty-day program. I went through it. It worked. I was very grateful for the massive changes in my life. But I had never considered doing a firewalk.

Despite the fear welling up in me, of course I said, "Oh, yeah, sure, the firewalk. That should be really fun. It should be interesting." But in reality I was thinking, *No way in hell. That is not going to happen. I am not doing that. That is stupid. That is crazy. There's no reason to do that. I mean, come on, why would anyone do that?*

The self-talk continued all the way up to the first day of the event. We arrived and took our seats. Tony hit the stage at about three o'clock in the afternoon, and (pardon the pun) he was on fire! Next thing I knew, it was one o'clock in the morning—ten hours later—and all three thousand of us were heading outside on a beautiful summer night. There was a big bonfire burning over on one side, but I was still holding my ground. *I'm not going to walk on fire. It's not going to happen. I'm sure that's only for the crazy people. Not everybody is going to firewalk.*

I stood all the way at the back, as far back as I could stand without leaving the event. I was the wallflower in the shadows of the gymnasium at the school dance. Up where the action was, many wheelbarrows full of coals had been dumped into lanes, and people were lined up facing each lane, waiting their turn. Everybody was really intense, yelling, "Yes! Yes! Yes!" But I was thinking, *No! No! No! No, it's not going to happen. No, I have nothing to prove here.*

A guy came up to me and said, "Hey, how are you doing? Are you going to walk tonight?"

"Absolutely not," I replied.

He smiled and said, "Hey, that's not a problem. We don't want you to do anything that you don't want to do. But wouldn't you at least like to watch?"

The question stopped me in my tracks. I answered, "Yeah, I really would."

"Well, then all you need to do is get in line, and eventually you'll get up close and you'll be able to see."

And then somehow I was in line. Soon I got to a position where I could see them walking. All these different people—men and women, short and tall, younger and older—they were all walking.

I was fascinated, mesmerized. I was just blown away.

Then somebody came up to me and said in my ear, "He knows when you're ready. When he says go, you go."

Suddenly, I realized I was next in line. I was staring down at the lane of coals. And my feet. Over the roar of the supporting crowd, this guy yelled, "Step up!"

I could feel the heat of the fire pushing me away, pulling me in. I was thinking to myself, *You've got to be kidding me.* But also, *This is my freaking chance.*

The guy yelled to me, "Eyes up! Keep your eyes up! Squeeze your fist and say yes!"

I squeezed my fist and I said, "Yes."

"Stronger!" he yelled.

"Yes," I said, a little louder.

"Stronger!"

I screamed, "Yes!" and next he yelled, "Go! Go! Go!"

I took off.

The next thing I knew, a couple guys are catching me, saying, "Stop! Wipe your feet! Celebrate!"

Stop. Wipe your feet. Celebrate.

A girl grabbed me by the shirt, pulling me out of line. "You did it, you did it, you did it!" she cried out.

I must have looked confused. "I did it. I did it," I replied. "What? I did what? No, I didn't . . ." Conflict raged in my head. I looked back at the lane of red coals behind me and muttered, "Holy crap, I just did it."

My next thought was, *You must have burned the hell out of yourself.*

I waited for the pain that I knew would come. Yet I didn't feel any pain. I looked at my feet, and there was nothing. I didn't have any burns.

As I said before, my next thoughts were, *What just happened? How did I do that?* These were followed by that question rising up inside me: *If I can firewalk, what else can I do?*

*****

That firewalk was the pivotal shift that changed my thinking and, consequently, my life. Somehow it leverages people out of the routines and habits that are getting them nowhere, and gets them to change their belief system about fear. A friend once explained it to me like this: You face everything and rise, or you forget everything and run. Either way, you move forward.

After my first firewalk, I joined the volunteer crew and soon found myself working for the Anthony Robbins Companies as a subcontractor in 1997. I became the assistant fire captain in 2003, and then was offered the position of fire captain. I accepted that role and started traveling around the world, leading enormous fire teams. I'd have fifty to sixty volunteers come and work with me to help facilitate each firewalk. My team and I safely took more than a quarter million people through firewalking. I've been firewalking now for almost twenty years, and I've had the honor and the privilege to work as a facilitator for all types of folks, from big names to average Joes.

But it wasn't until I came to the Firewalking Institute and met Charles that I finally understood the depths there are to firewalking—the different lengths and what they mean, the different elements of transformation, the different levels of personal development. The extraordinary training and fear-based exercises that Charles offers are second to none. I thought I knew quite a bit about firewalking—after all, I'd done it for so long. But everything changed once I got to know

Charles and to truly understand the science behind firewalking and the relationship a person can have with the fire. Now I can do "firestanding"—stand on the coals for minutes at a time. I have done a "108": walked a ten-foot lane 108 times in one session. These are things I never would've thought possible in the past.

I've watched thousands of transformations in my lifetime. I've seen what it does for people. I've seen what it does for their families. I've even seen what it did for my own children. My daughter was eight years old and my son, eleven. Their firewalk meant the building of a foundation for them, an inspiration and a lesson about what's possible in life. So many young people are told what they can't do and why they can't do it. I raised my kids the opposite way, always telling them, "You can do whatever you put your mind to." They're young adults now, and firewalking still has a profound impact on them today. Both are successful firewalkers, and my son is now one of the youngest certified firewalkers in the world. My goal was to raise the bar by inspiring them from an early age to think, *I am capable of some very powerful things.*

I've seen many people influenced by the positive paradigm shift that happens during a firewalk event. Firewalking is huge today. Corporate America is recognizing its benefits. People of all professions use firewalking today as a way to shift their thinking and to change their belief systems about who they are and what they're truly capable of. We've walked everybody from corporate dads and soccer moms to professional athletes to Usher, Oprah, Anthony Hopkins, Kiefer Sutherland, and other celebrities. Most firewalkers never become a professional athlete or a major actor on the big screen. But for that instant, when it's their turn to walk, they shine like any star on Broadway. There's a real profound moment as you look down at those coals. As you take that first step, and then when you get to the other side, you discover what it's like to feel that fear, embrace that fear, and move beyond that fear. You literally take your life to another level.

The nineteen lessons of this book can bring your life to another level, too. I should know: I learned more from firewalking at a four-day event with Charles Horton's Firewalking Institute of Research and Education (F.I.R.E.) than I did in ten years with even the wonderful Anthony Robbins Companies. Charles Horton has a story to tell, a story that contains important, valuable lessons for life and business—and he's not the only one. We all have a story. Some of us have some pretty creative stories: *I'm too old. I'm too young. I don't have the time. I don't have the money. I don't have the education. I don't have the background. I don't have the resources.*

Stop!

The lessons in this book will help you see behind the story you tell yourself about your life. You'll learn that the reason we don't have something powerful in our lives is we're constantly telling ourselves a story about why we can't have it. I equate that to the self-talk I experienced before my first firewalk, standing in line and listening to your head saying you can't do it. The struggles you've faced start to bubble up.

What struggles are an ongoing part of your life?

The lessons in this book will help you identify, move past, and even ease or eliminate those struggles.

When you get close to taking the first step onto that bed of coals, you hear, "He knows when you're ready. When he says go, you go." It relieves you of the responsibility of making that decision.

Where else in your life have you given away your power?

The lessons in this book will help you recognize who holds the power to change your life—and ensure that person is you.

I've watched many hundreds of thousands of people firewalk. I've learned that if they take the first step, they'll definitely take the second, third, fourth, fifth, sixth, and so on, because now it's about getting to the other side. That first step is quite literally to step forward—to take action. And to do so, they must overcome their own particular brand of fear, whatever it may be. The fear that I had about firewalking was the exact same fear I've had about other things in my life: about relationships, about starting my own business, about getting married and having a family.

What's your fear?

Whatever it is, I'm here to tell you that it's not insurmountable. The lessons in this book will help you begin to face your fears and to counteract them. You just have to take that first step. Taking the first step is monumental. You are reclaiming your power to go ahead and do it—to do the firewalk, to bite the bullet and take charge of your life.

The result is a transformation that is profound beyond words. And then it's time to stop, wipe your feet, and celebrate! The celebration integrates your new commitment, your new connection, your new mission. The celebration, in my opinion, helps create your "why."

People whom I've assisted in firewalking tell me stories about how it all started with taking that first step. They've elevated their life to a place where they are completely different today. Their belief systems are completely changed. They're no longer under the spell of inaction. They no longer allow themselves to continue being programmed by their parents, peer group, colleagues, or relatives. Instead of making excuses or believing that they couldn't do something, they've taken action and changed their stories. Even people who have been bombarded in life with extreme circumstances have changed their future. With lessons like those presented in this book, you can change yours, too.

What is your firewalk? What is your struggle on the way up to the line? Who tells you when you're ready? Who tells you when to go? What is your new commitment to the first step? What is your "why" of significance to celebrate? This book is your first step toward finding the answers to these questions and more—and toward living the life you want to lead.

Find a time and a place to firewalk. Make that commitment to walk. Take that first step toward the rest of your life's journey. And then . . . stop. Wipe your feet. Celebrate!

—Dave Albin

Firewalking Institute of Research and Education
(F.I.R.E.) Master Firewalking Instructor
Former Anthony Robbins Companies
Fire Captain (for a decade)
One of the world's most experienced firewalkers

Introduction

Igniting the Secret

Have you ever walked through fire?

Yes, I am talking about fire—a red-hot, twelve-hundred-degree bed of coals—though people face many types of "fires" in their personal and professional lives, from skydiving or swimming with sharks to asking for a promotion or starting their own business. Many kinds of activities can stretch a person's comfort level and force a person to face his or her fears. Both a real fire and a symbolic fire offer a hidden gift, the perfect opportunity, bestowing on each person the lesson he or she needs the most.

Sometimes people are aware of what they need. Other times they think they know what they need, or they think they need nothing. But fire is omnipotent, and it reveals the truth. No matter what people believe when they come to the fire, what they receive at the fire is a life-changing breakthrough.

Whether the fire you face is a real one or not, confronting adversity and challenge is a part of life that makes you stronger. When you walk through fire, you face your fears and limitations, and you come out victorious on the other side.

This book is going to help you do just that, whether you are seeking greater health, wealth, or happiness—and whether you choose a path that walks through real fires or symbolic ones.

I am constantly reminded of the power of fire by the thousands and thousands of individuals I have led across the coals. In my firewalk sessions, people learn how to actually walk on hot coals, and it opens up so much in their lives. It helps them overcome fear, transform their thinking, and break through barriers that have been holding them back.

The first night I crossed the coals, I thought it was all about the fire. I thought it was about stepping up and proving what you can do. Sure, that is a part of it. But as my life and career have developed, and as my firewalking skills have improved, I've learned that firewalking is so much more. I've realized that for me, the fire has always been not just about my experience, but also about guiding someone else through it.

I've realized that I am a teacher. It's my calling.

But it wasn't my first calling.

I have been entrepreneurial all my life—and a business owner since I was eighteen. In fact, I have owned (and still own) multiple businesses, and now I'm a public speaker who presents my ideas on being a successful entrepreneur to companies around the country and the globe. So how did I become a teacher? And how did becoming a teacher lead me to writing this book?

Throughout my life, I've embarked on many great adventures. Some of them have changed my life. They've helped me develop a number of useful, insightful business theories and life lessons. But what's really behind these practical philosophies is a set of methods that allow me to face my fears and control my destiny. What I've learned from my greatest adventures—and from firewalking in particular—are the strategies that guide my life. And now I want to share them with you.

I learned about firewalking at a seminar in the early 2000s led by Tony Robbins, one of America's greatest teachers. I went to the seminar with no fear of firewalking—no opinion about it at all, in fact. After watching the large bonfire burn, however, I chickened out. It wouldn't be the last time.

I attended the firewalk seminar not once, but a half dozen times over as many years. It was frustrating. I was accustomed to succeeding. Why had I failed at this? Why could I conquer every area of life but not conquer a fear that I didn't even know I had?

As an entrepreneur, I had walked through a lot of fires. Not literally, of course. But when you make the decision to pave your own way—to start a business and live a life of freedom—there are a lot of challenges to overcome. Some days you might not be able to make payroll. Other days you hit an obstacle that you didn't see coming and don't know how to get around. On others still, an employee might quit or let you down.

What fires have you walked through, in business and in life? Have you lost your job or felt dissatisfied with your career? Have you suffered from health problems or other difficulties? Have you lost someone or seen an important relationship fail? These are the fires we experience every day in life.

What fires have you backed away from—and do those fires still haunt you?

Even though I'd given in to that initial fear and backed out on my first firewalk, I knew that I would need to conquer this obstacle. It haunted me, and I knew I had to overcome it. Perseverance is an important trait when it comes to building a business or rising above a personal obstacle. You've got to be able to overcome your fear, to try again, to keep on walking. Pressure leads to growth, and it's a part of every successful entrepreneur's life.

Finally, tired of that incredible weight on my shoulders, I contacted the Firewalking Institute of Research and Education (F.I.R.E.), a company that had trained hundreds of firewalk instructors around the globe. F.I.R.E. at the time did not offer frequent courses, but the company founder referred me to John Maisel, whom I hired to conduct a firewalk for several dozen people from my company. After setting up the event, I was still thinking about the what-ifs. In fact, I was totally terrified. For weeks, if I even thought of the upcoming challenge, my body would revolt. I would shiver and become physically ill. But I have a cynical side, and I thought there had to be a trick.

The day before the firewalk, John showed up at my house with his fire tender, Ted Shaw, and we went to dinner. Throughout our meeting I was focused only on the firewalk. To this day, I don't remember anything else that we discussed.

"What's the trick?" I asked at last. "What's the secret?"

"Oh, there's no trick," John replied, smiling calmly. "No secret. The coals are really twelve hundred degrees." He then changed the subject.

The next day was horrible. Stress, fear, and panic followed me all day. When it came time to walk, I jumped up and down near the fire, trying to build myself up—to raise my internal state to where I could make the walk. I stayed there for a little while. My employees were all watching, but still I could not move. I was overcome with anxiety.

John came up beside me. "There's a nice path. Go for it."

I don't know how he did it, but I guess that's why he's so good at what he does. Anyway, I took that first step—it's the hard one—and the rest came easy.

I did it!

After finally walking across the coals, I went to a place by myself and cried for a full five minutes. I was in shock. Getting across that fire was such a big deal for me. I had built this fear up so big in my mind, and made it so difficult for so long, but in the end it was so easy. I felt as if five thousand pounds had fallen off my shoulders.

Aren't most of our fears like that? They're not real, just built up in our heads. Our greatest fears are in our mind. But when we finally conquer them, whatever we feared becomes so easy! That's a big lesson I learned from firewalking. Most of the fears and limitations we hold on to are self-imposed.

In my seminars today, I ask, "Who has walked on fire?"

A murmur goes through the audience: Some have, and some haven't.

Then, to explain the feeling of firewalking, I ask, "Has anyone ever walked on or skipped across really hot sand?"

Lots of heads nod.

"It's nothing like that!" I say. "Has anyone ever walked barefooted on asphalt? You know, the hot, nearly bubbly kind?"

Lots of heads nod again.

"It's nothing like that!" I say again. Then I tell them that for me, firewalking "in state"—emotionally charged, in peak form, 100 percent focused—is like walking on cool popcorn. I don't feel the fire at all, because I'm in a different state of mind.

Twenty years ago scientists believed that firewalking was possible because of the Leidenfrost effect, like when you lick your fingers and quickly touch an iron or skillet. You hear a sizzle, but your skin is fine—no burn. The theory was that you would sweat before firewalking, or, before you walked, the instructor would toss water on the ground before the coals, which creates a layer of moisture or vapor that prevents the soles of the feet from fully contacting the coals. But that's not it at all. As time went on, scientists saw that not all instructors put water on the ground before the coals before the walk, and that not all people sweat. Even if you do sweat, it would evaporate by the end of a longer walk across the fire.

Now scientists say that the conductivity theory is the reason firewalking is possible—that the coals (like air) are poor conductors and so cannot burn your feet. But I've seen a person walk across a great conductor—a glowing red, metal grill laid over the coals—without injury, even when their footprints remain on the metal. Nor does the conductivity theory explain why some people can stand on the coals for upward of five minutes without getting burned. Or why, on the same walk at the same speed, some get "kisses" (blisters) and some don't.

I believe that the power to walk on fire is in your belief. It doesn't matter what you want to do in life, and it doesn't matter what people say. You have the power within you to find out for yourself what is possible. Your belief system is everything. How you think impacts everything else in your life: your actions, your heart, and your relationships.

If you want to achieve something—if you're facing a fire in your life, or if a past fire still haunts your life dreams—you simply have to conquer your fears and do it. You just have to ignite the secret: that you have the ability to conquer your limitations.

This book offers the lessons that are the foundation of a successful life and business. Thanks to these lessons, which I've learned while in business, while firewalking and experiencing other intense situations, and in running the Firewalking Institute of Research and Education (F.I.R.E.), I've been able to live a life of freedom—and you can, too. I've grown as an entrepreneur and as a person, avoiding some of the common pitfalls and poor decisions that other people make—and you can, too. After decades of paving my own way and building businesses from the ground up, I've learned (sometimes the hard way) what to do and what not to do.

You can, too.

But what I've taken away from firewalking is not just a set of lessons—it's a group of strategies you can apply and traits you can cultivate in order to become successful. In fact, these nineteen strategies are used by the most successful people in the world, and they will ignite your life and business.

Each lesson occupies its own "chapter," and the chapter order is loosely chronological based on how someone ideally might react to a challenging situation. Each chapter presents a personal or professional story from my life (or from the lives of mentors along the way), intended to clarify the lesson and how I learned it, as well as what it means for you and how to apply it. Finally, each lesson reinforces the message via simple, effective takeaways that you can use to consider your unique scenario and go deeper into the practice of that particular strategy.

The nineteen lessons you are about to encounter will help you walk through any fire, real or perceived.

For many people, an experience like the firewalk generates a huge shift in life. Igniting the secret of the firewalk—that you *can* conquer your fears and stop creating mental limitations—will help you clear away fears and self-doubt, shift your perspective on life, focus on your intentions and goals, stoke your internal fire, and overcome any challenges. It will encourage you to see opportunities rather than obstacles—to forge your path forward through any bed of coals. Just imagine what you'll be able to accomplish!

Now it's time to take that first step . . .

Take Action

When I teach firewalking, I joke, "You don't need to be great to start, but you need to start to be great." Firewalking—just like achieving any goal in life—is all about putting one foot in front of the other. You have to cross that bed of coals. Thinking and talking about it leads nowhere.

The first step in a new direction is going to be the hardest. Some say you should set your intentions, plan things out, do a little self-exploration, and so forth before taking any action. But any true entrepreneur knows action comes first. Spend too much time in your head and you'll never get to where you want to be.

The only measure of success is whether you take action on your ideas.

Take Three Steps to Success

How many times have you seen or heard about someone who had a great idea or a business they never followed through on? Did that person achieve his or her dreams with the idea alone? No.

Successful people take action. They've achieved success through a series of steps that lead to their ultimate goal. It's not enough just to think about your dream. You've got to act on it.

If you're reading this book, you know that it's time.

There are three important steps to achieve anything in your life, from an enlightening firewalk to a successful job or business venture to a fulfilling relationship. I will come back to these three steps again and again throughout the lessons and strategies revealed in this book.

The first step is *awareness*. You must be aware of where you are—both externally and internally aware.

The second step is *willingness*. To reach your goals, especially the long-term ones, you must be and stay committed. Only through ongoing willingness to commit can you achieve your lifelong dreams.

And the third step—perhaps the most important, and the one I want to discuss in this Lesson No. 1—is *action*. Massive and consistent action.

Your success is linked to the positive action you take. It's more than just planning and envisioning your success. You can't be successful if you simply sit around and talk. You need to do something. As an entrepreneur, you've got to take action.

I've been in the personal development industry for decades, and I've seen thousands of people go to the seminars and get all pumped up. But then they walk out those doors and back into their own world, and their lives don't change at all. They don't act on what they've learned.

You can't get what you want if you refuse to step out of your neat little bubble and do the dirty work.

I'm constantly taking steps toward achieving my goals. Many times, of course, I take steps that don't work. But then I take more steps until I find a way to make it work. Even if things don't work out, I keep trying. I keep taking action.

If you stop or stand still, that's when failure happens.

This is how I run my life, and it's also how I run my companies. I take action to surround myself with a smart and enthusiastic team. We are constantly changing what we do, doing new things, and trying to market ourselves in unique ways. We encourage our employees to figure out new ways to work and to market, and we test these ideas and check the results. Then we implement what works best. We keep moving forward.

I'm on my sixth venture right now.

When I start companies, I try to be the catalyst. I help get things going, nurture my employees to succeed and deliver, delegate various aspects of the company to my trusted team, and then go find something else that needs doing. I'm someone who wants to keep constantly moving on to new businesses, new ambitions, new dreams. Constant action is at the core of my success, both in business and in life.

If you think about it, you can't finish the race, or, in fact, even start the race, if you don't enter the race.

Speaking of races, how many times have you heard a friend say, "I have a goal. I want to lose ten pounds. I want to enter a 5K run." A few months go by, and then a few years, but no 5K happens and those ten pounds are joined by ten more. How many of your friends actually achieve the goals they're talking about? Sure, some have, but many never do, because they don't take action.

Put your best foot forward, and take that leap. When you take action, great things are going to happen.

Balance Action with Analysis

About fifteen years ago, when I was already in the check guarantee business, somebody came to me and said, "You should enter into the short-term loan business. People need the money."

I thought it was a good idea. So I started a store and tried it out. When I ran into the man who'd advised me to start in the business, he was still talking about it and analyzing every possible outcome. He had done nothing. Meanwhile, five years later, I had twenty stores going very successfully!

And still my friend failed to take action. He decided it was too late into the evolution of the business model to get started. Well, it wasn't too late. I continued to grow to more than seventy stores. I call his approach "paralysis through analysis." As an entrepreneur, I take action sometimes with almost no thought at all, while my friend analyzes things too much. He debates the possibilities but seldom takes that leap.

I tell this story all the time to explain what happens when you fail to take action. In my opinion, this friend just studied the idea too much. That's his nature. It's also not a good idea to enter into something or start a company blindly. I've acted too fast several times and cost myself a lot of money.

I once decided to sell and finance computers through FastBucks, my chain of short-term loan stores. At the time, I had surrounded myself with "yes-men." I did not have a staff that would stand up to me or offer advice that counterbalanced my own ideas. So I jumped right in and started the process of selling computers, with no ability to track and control the sales or inventory. I lost millions.

Another time I decided to get into the used-car business. Acting too quickly and lacking good advice once again, I hired a thief to run the business. I didn't have the necessary controls in place. I lost millions.

So, taking action is good, but balancing your weaknesses is good, too. That's why my friend who analyzes everything is now my executive vice president at Fast-Bucks. Together we make a great team.

Creating a good team is important (as I will explain further in Lesson No. 4). You need to take action, but you also need to do the homework. Surround yourself with a team that balances action with analysis, to ensure you don't misstep. Let them analyze, and you can be the one who drives and pushes people to achieve. Listen to their insights and information, and then decide how to act. But whatever idea you decide to act on, just do it.

Hard work involves a series of actions like this. It's more than just planning. You have to act.

Every successful person I know has developed a routine of taking successful action. There is no secret. It's not magical thinking. The truth is, successful people have specific habits that they carry out each day in order to be successful. The most important habit is taking action. You've got to use it—or lose it.

I once hired a new district manager for FastBucks, and he was bringing in big numbers over everyone else. He was running 25 or 30 percent more in revenues over the previous year, and yet when he came in with an idea that he wanted to try, I cut him down. I said, "We've already done this four times in this company, and it has not worked!"

He was very respectful in the meeting. He didn't resist me or say anything negative. But when he took me aside later to talk about all of his prior and current successes, he said, "You know, there are things that people have said not to try here, so I haven't tried them. But this time I would like to try it myself, because I think I can make it work."

I thought about his logic, and finally I said, "Go for it! Do it your way and let's see your results." After all, his approach was like mine: Just try something, and see what works. He had convinced me that he could do it. He wanted to keep up his habit of taking action. He did, and his idea was a success.

Just thinking about taking action won't get you very far in life.

Taking action is how you begin down the path of success.

Personal Practice: Taking Action

What actions would you take to achieve your goals if you had no fear?

What things will you take action on in the next six months?

Manage the Details

In my seminars, I sometimes lead an exercise where the participants walk barefoot on broken glass. Walking on broken glass is very different from firewalking. In firewalking, the first step is the hardest one, and the rest come easily and quickly.

In glass-walking, you must walk very slowly and with absolute mindfulness, paying close attention to every shift of your foot. If you stay on top of the glass, you're going to be fine. You can avoid the big shards, so they likely won't be the ones to cut you. But if you're not careful, the little ones might.

Glass is the perfect way to illustrate that it's the small stuff that gets you. By walking on broken glass, I've learned to pay attention to those teeny-tiny little shards. As the saying goes, *The devil is in the details.*

Do Sweat the Small Stuff

There's another old saying you've probably heard: *Don't sweat the small stuff.* Like a lot of false words and quotes, taking this to heart has caused the destruction of many. Not sweating the small stuff is fine when it comes to an approach to managing stress. But if you don't manage the details of your life, you'll find yourself surrounded by a lot more stress.

We absolutely should pay attention to the small things. Sure, we don't have to sweat constantly over them, but small issues must be attended to before they spiral out of control and become big issues.

Manage the details—or they could be your downfall.

I learned this lesson once in an exhilarating way on an adventure in Africa, when I spent some time among lions. I have been on about forty safaris now, logging 150 hours of searching for and viewing African big game. Of course, I always want to go further with things I benefit from or enjoy. So I decided to volunteer at a lion farm, where I got to work with and learn from about ninety lions.

The person who managed the lion farm showed us how we should approach lions of all ages. Eager to immerse myself in the experience, I didn't sweat what I considered the "small stuff" in this presentation. I went ahead and tried to bottle-feed a six-month-old cub, ignoring a seemingly minor detail: the three other larger, hungrier cubs who all wanted the milk, too.

As I fed the smallest lion cub, the other cubs circled around me, eyes focused on the bottle. The small cub noticed, and was going to ensure she got it all. She squirmed and lashed out, and in the process mauled my arms pretty good.

After washing up and tending to my bleeding arms, I pulled myself together and went back to the kitchen. My friend was there waiting for me, holding a newly filled bottle. I was still in pain and now a bit shocked: I'd thought I was done, but now I had to go among the lions all over again.

Not wanting to cause more damage to myself, this time I paid attention to the details of my surroundings. I scooped up the small cub, taking her to a private enclosure to feed her. Then I chose to sit in an area that necessitated her standing on all fours, rather than lean against me, to maintain her balance.

Success! I was no longer a scratching post for these big kittens.

The lesson: Sweat the small stuff (feeding milk to an overgrown kitten), or it could quickly turn into big stuff (feeding yourself to the lions). It's true in life, and it's true in business. One overlooked detail can get you killed—or at the very least, mauled—in the marketplace as in the jungle.

When seeking the path of success in your personal and professional life, leave no stone unturned. Keep your eyes wide open for details large and small.

Don't Overlook the Details

While driving, have you ever had a small detail—a soft tire, an expired inspection sticker, an overlooked speed limit sign—lead to a problem on the road or even a ticket? I know plenty of people who have. They didn't pay attention to the details, and those details came back to haunt them, impacting their mobility and their pocketbook.

I've seen a lot of successful people miss details that have impacted their business or even their direction in life. Overlooking the following four details in particular can spell disaster in any business situation and in quite a few personal ones.

Detail No. 1: Get in your peak state.

In order to be successful, first you need to be "in state"—you have to be at your emotional peak, entirely focused on the situation at hand. You must be excited. You must be ready. You must be willing. You must be motivated. And you must believe in yourself, your abilities, and your objective.

I was doing the glass-walk seminar one time for a group of unemployed financial professionals, and right at the start I asked whether the attendees really, truly wanted a job. After a few confused looks, most of them answered yes, of course they did. But it's not enough to simply say that you want a new job (or a new business, a new client, or whatever the case may be). You must be enthused and motivated by the job, and you have to believe the job is yours.

If you go into an interview and you're feeling down and miserable, that will come through to your interviewers. If you're starting a business but you just don't feel confident about getting it off the ground, your consumers and competitors will notice. It may seem to be a small detail, but that extra energy, that extra bit of confidence you exude, will be the edge you need to nudge out the competition. It does not matter what state the economy is in. It does not matter what is happening in your particular industry right now. Good companies are always, always looking for winners. Talk to the right people, and convince them of your worth, and they will create a position for you.

It may seem like a minor detail, because being at your peak is hard to quantify. But getting your head in the game—getting "in state"—is crucial to success in any professional or personal enterprise. (I will come back to this in Lesson No. 10.)

Detail No. 2: Do your research.

If you're looking to make a change, you need to have your "house" in order. A big detail that many people in business (including myself) fail to address is doing the research necessary to create a proper business plan. That plan can be as simple as stating the company's financial goals or outlining its key mission, or as detailed as putting a step-by-step plan in place to ensure a successful year. A proper business plan will show that there is a way to get profitable. It makes you think through all the expenses. It shows that you know how much time and money it will take to get profitable. And in business, naturally, profit is the bottom line.

If you're looking for a new job, like the unemployed people at my glass-walk seminar, research the interviewer and the company. This applies to any situation when you're interacting with other people and hoping to come away successful in achieving your goals, whether you're in sales or simply trying to make an impression on a personal acquaintance. Show that you're not just going through the motions. Create rapport with the individual by knowing something about them. If you went to the same college or attend the same church, bingo! Or maybe you share a hobby, like running or cycling or knitting or whatever. If you can't find out anything about the person online, ask their assistant. If all else fails, ask your interviewer.

I'll be honest: doing this kind of legwork doesn't come naturally to me. It's not my forte, and perhaps it's not yours either. This is where that first step we talked about earlier comes in: awareness. How well do you know yourself? I know myself well enough to know I'm never going to create a business plan. So I don't sweat it. Instead, I have someone else do it for me. If researching the background of a person or a company isn't your thing, find someone to manage these details for you. Hire someone who can handle this with aplomb, even if you have to pay your sister.

Remember, it's those tiny budget lines and other overlooked details that will get you if they're neglected for too long. Dot your *i*'s and cross your *t*'s. Details matter!

Detail No. 3: Ask for what you want.

During the speech to unemployed financial professionals I referenced earlier, I also told them I happened to be looking for a chief financial officer for one of my businesses. After the presentation, half a dozen people came up to me and said, "Hi, I'm your CFO." They had pumped themselves up, gotten "in state," and had the courage to approach me—detail number one, accomplished. Some of them had done their research and found a way to connect with me—detail number two.

I greeted each person and handed him or her my business card. What do you think happened? Not one person followed up. These people claimed they wanted to make a change but failed to address this essential detail by taking action.

If you see what you want and you're truly interested in going for it, then take that extra step and ask for it. Failing to ask for what you want or neglecting to follow up indicates that you aren't really sure whether you want to move forward. For someone supposedly seeking success, this is a sad state of affairs. It shows a lack of intention and a lack of willingness (the second step to success I mentioned in Lesson No. 1).

Detail No. 4: Say thank you.

Finally, it is vital to express your thanks to those with whom you come in contact, be they colleagues or competitors, peers or superiors, new acquaintances or old. As I told the unemployed glass-walkers, sending an appreciative card could mean the difference in whether an interviewer remembers you. And quite frankly, it's just a simple way of highlighting your integrity and professionalism.

This so-called detail is overlooked all too often today, in business and in the world at large. Perhaps it's something we've failed to emphasize in our modern culture. And don't make the mistake of thinking an e-mailed thank-you or a form letter has the same impact as a handwritten letter, hand-delivered or sent by next-day air. Each time I visit my favorite restaurant, Del Frisco's, I get a handwritten thank-you card from the server. It's a nice touch, and it ensures that I drive by many other steakhouses to go to Del Frisco's. It's above and beyond customer service. I get treated like royalty each time I go there. The handwritten, not preprinted, card goes a long way to keep them in my mind.

But for a minor detail, saying a simple "thank you" really packs a punch. In all sorts of situations, among all sorts of people—a new boss, a potential client, a group of consumers, a valued vendor or service provider, and especially someone who could give you that big break you're seeking—a little gratefulness goes a long way.

These four details are simple but important, and so intrinsic that we tend to overlook them. Do so at your peril.

Personal Practice: Managing the Details

What details do you have to manage in your finances, health, life, home, or business?

What happens when you fail to pay attention to the details? How have you learned from such mistakes?

Lesson No. 3
Find Out What Is Possible

Sometimes we have to accept reality and just work within those boundaries—but many more times, I've found, we must push the limits and adjust those boundaries ourselves. A client in Spain reminded me of this once. I had already trained three people in Spain to firewalk, and my latest client there wanted me to go to Spain to teach him and his staff. But this would bring an extra concern, above and beyond the usual worries for first-timers: open fires were illegal in Spain.

I told my client, Enrique Juardo, about the other firewalkers' experiences in Spain. I felt it was only right to warn him that they had told me open fires were technically forbidden in his country.

He waved away my concern. "I got it covered," he said.

He was right—I needn't have worried. Enrique certainly didn't. He managed to rent space at a Catholic retreat center that had a lot of land and influence. They wanted Enrique's business, and they acquired the proper permission to have open fires.

Since then, Enrique has firewalked thousands of times, and now he teaches others to do so, just as I did for him that first time. In fact, he has trained more than two hundred people in Spain who regularly hold firewalks all over the country. He is the most successful promoter the Firewalking Institute of Research and Education (F.I.R.E.) has ever had. He has taught me a lot about believing in yourself and figuring out for yourself what can be done.

Deny the Impossible

Growing up, we are taught sayings like *It takes money to make money* and *The rich get richer, and the poor get poorer.* What a bunch of baloney. Most of these sayings must have been thought up by people with a poverty mind-set. That's not you. You don't have to believe them.

The truth is, you don't need money, elite connections, or even a strong education to create success. No matter where you are in business or in your personal life, to achieve success you simply have to hold on to your convictions about what is possible.

That's right: only you can determine what is possible in your life.

I can't tell you how many times I've been told that I'm not good at something or that I can't do something, and I've just ignored it and stayed focused. (I'll get into greater depth about staying focused in Lesson No. 5.) Much of my success in life has happened when I refused to believe what other people were saying.

Once I found something I wanted to do, I denied that it was impossible. Instead, I learned for myself what was possible.

In high school I shared a room in a mobile home with my stepbrother. We were rather poor. After high school I moved from Austin, Texas, to Dallas with a friend to start a martial arts school. All that came with me were a few boxes of clothes and a $500 Chevy Chevette. I had barely graduated high school. I didn't have the education or the money supposedly needed to start a business. But at twenty years old, I started my first business: SmartCheck, which the *Nielsen Report* in 1998 called the eighth-largest check verification and guarantee company in the world.

I began by doing just check collections. Then, because I didn't want to lose business, I moved up to check verification. But I would lose customers because I did not do check guarantee, so I started doing that business as well.

Well, my competitors in the guarantee business thought you had to have millions and millions of dollars behind you or you couldn't successfully do check guarantee. Thank God, I didn't know that when I started, because I would have never been able to pull it off. So what did I do?

I just found a way.

Most of my competitors bought checks after seven days, in which case you did have to have more up-front money. So I changed that seven days into forty-five days. This extended period of time allowed me to collect 90 to 95 percent of the checks that I was going to collect. I had to pay only for the checks that I couldn't collect. And thanks to the fee I was charging, I was able to do that. Making just that little bit of a change to the product allowed me to do what everyone else said couldn't be done.

Instead of simply accepting that something was impossible, I had found out for myself what could and couldn't be done.

I have been going to the same excellent African safari lodge now for some time. Sitting in a vehicle watching the pride of lions just yards away, I asked if we could go back and walk with them. I was told that if I were to leave the vehicle, I would be dead. "We never walk alongside lions with cubs," said the guide. "Very dangerous. Most animals will kill to protect their young." Made sense to me!

But I kept wanting to do a walking safari, and finally the lodge owner helped me arrange it. The anticipation grew and grew—until I was told that our intention was *not* to encounter wild animals, but simply to enjoy a nature walk. Guides are not allowed to usher guests into intentionally dangerous animal interactions. Also, there were tons of rules: No talking—only natural sounds allowed. Walk single file at a normal pace—never run. If you run, you are food. If you drop something, don't pick it up. Otherwise, follow the guide's lead.

Still, it was fun. We did see some elephants at a distance—but none of the dangerous buffalo, hippos, or lions. So I scheduled another walk—just me, the lodge owner, and two guides. After walking for about an hour, we crossed our path and the guide noticed fresh lion prints. She then asked if I wanted to track the lions.

"Hell, yes!" I said.

When you are tracking an animal, you can see the prints in soft sand, but when the ground is hard you can lose the tracks. We fanned out separately to look for the tracks in different directions and spoke loudly to update each other on our findings. An hour passed, and finally we came upon the two cutest little cubs, right there in front of us on the ground.

Wait, I thought. *That's not good.* The rule was, don't go near the cubs! We were walking in a single file line again. Two guides in the front, owner in the middle, me in the back. Then I saw Mama Lion. After almost running, I froze, stared at the lioness, and snapped my fingers for the guides to know. They moved in front of me and shouted, "*Stop, don't run!*" I rolled my eyes, thinking, *I called them.* For what seemed like an eternity, the lioness looked at us. We looked at her. The tension mounted. Then she laid her head down, as did the four others that I had just noticed surrounding us.

The guide told me later that provided you don't run, 80 percent of the time lions do exactly what they did—check you out, then ignore you. About 16 percent of the time they run away. And about 4 percent of the time, they will charge you but stop right in front of you. After the trek, the guides told me they never even loaded their guns. Of course, there are exceptions when someone does get killed by a lion, but that is rare.

I was told that walking with lions was impossible—that if I left the vehicle, I would be eaten. Yet it wasn't true. I was told that I had to walk and talk a certain way, or I would be in danger. Yet it wasn't true. I was told that if I encountered lion cubs, the mother would try to attack. Yet it wasn't true. In the end, I walked with lions, and I encountered cubs, and I lived to tell the story. The fact of the matter was that when we were quiet and sneaking around, the mother wanted to know what we were up to. Once we made noise, the lions went about their naps and ignored us. The moral: find out for yourself what is true.

Believe in Yourself

When you're fighting for success in business and in life, the most powerful weapon in your arsenal is not your gift or talent (spectacular though it may be), or even your ideas or words (clever as they may be). It's your belief system.

Even the most gifted, ingenious human will not achieve success unless that person believes they can be successful. You have to be willing to overcome the naysayers and obstacles, so that once you believe you can do something, it becomes possible.

Belief linked to action is important. So what if another person doesn't believe in you? You've got to move forward and believe in yourself.

For generations, the taxicab system has dominated the world. Who would have thought you could just download an app on your phone to call a cab—and that everybody would actually begin doing it, too? It sounded a bit crazy at first, but that didn't stop the guys who started Uber. If they had not thought outside of the box and believed in their idea, the world never would have seen this innovative transportation system. The driver tracking system is nothing short of brilliant: A driver who gets bad marks is automatically removed from the pool. The founders of Uber found out what people wanted—friendly, trustworthy cab drivers on demand—and then found out how to make it happen.

There are a lot of amazing businesses like that. Uber worked because some individuals believed in themselves enough to push forward. They sought what was possible and made it happen.

Belief in yourself is a powerful force, whether it allows you to stand on burning coals or start a multi-million-dollar business in your garage. If you believe you are capable of something, you will do it.

If you have a better way of doing business, don't kowtow to the people who insist, "We've always done it this way." Discover for yourself what is possible, and stick to your guns.

When I entered the check-verification business and everyone said I would need millions of dollars backing the process—well, that's what they thought. That was their way. But I believed in myself and my approach, and from the start, I knew I wouldn't operate my business their way.

Follow your convictions, in life as well as in business. When you believe something is possible, be determined. Stay focused and continue to believe in yourself, despite people who come along and tell you that you can't do it.

Do whatever it takes to develop the confidence to believe in yourself. Maybe firewalking or skydiving isn't your thing, but you find introspection in another activity: a personal fitness program, a group retreat, an educational course. Take the time and make the effort to get in touch with your beliefs, your values, and your inner strength.

When you know yourself, your goals, and your business, if you think something is possible, nothing can stop you.

Personal Practice: Finding Out What Is Possible

What do you believe in? What constitutes your belief system?

What is stopping you from taking action to achieve your dreams? How can you develop the confidence to believe in yourself?

Surround Yourself with Success

After I hired John Maisel to guide that first firewalk for my company, I immediately decided I had to learn more. I'm the type of person who feels like if you are going to do something, do it all the way. I continued firewalking at every opportunity. My next step was to become a firewalk instructor.

John agreed to do a private training for me, and eventually I became a firewalk instructor. But I had to follow my nature and continue moving up the ladder. I needed to go to the top and learn from the person who trained John.

So I attended one of the training sessions presented by the founder and head of the Firewalking Institute of Research and Education (F.I.R.E.). I soon found, however, that this man's approach was vastly different from mine. He would go off on long cussing sessions if you broke any of his rules. He made the fires so hot that most F.I.R.E. events led to someone being hospitalized. He believed you could not control the temperature of the fire and taught that if you got burned, it was a lesson from a higher power. I'm grateful that John had taught me otherwise, or today

I would not be sharing the great benefits that come from firewalking.

What's more, the founder was dishonest. He portrayed himself as being in constant danger of permanent paralysis because of a neck and spine injury, and claimed to need a special chair, yet alone with staff he would plop into any chair handy. He once locked himself out of a meeting room and elected to scale a high fence rather than wait for someone to let him back in. Another time he told me he planned to wear a neck brace to "even the playing field" with a potential adversary.

It became painfully clear that I was dealing with someone who wasn't a positive influence when, one day on a long hike, he walked rapidly and hopped over rocks and boulders, leaving two of us in the dust—despite his alleged spine injury and the fact that we were twenty years his junior. He spoke negatively, about some of my personal heroes and mentors in particular, and that didn't sit well with me at all. He shared some of his own life lessons that day—one was "Do it to the other guy before he does it to you."

Clearly, the founder was not my kind of guy. At this point I decided firewalking needed a new face.

That very opportunity arose when the founder of F.I.R.E. announced his retirement. I decided to buy the institute and make some changes to it. I needed to surround myself—and my new company—with optimism and success, not pessimism and contempt.

Eliminate Energy Drains

Are there people in your life who are nipping at your heels, lollygagging instead of being go-getters, or waiting to pounce on you should you stumble and fall? Get rid of them! Focus instead on people who soar and who encourage you to do the same. Find good coaches, mentors, and role models who will convince you that you can walk on hot coals and come out unscathed, not tell you to expect to get burned.

Eliminate the negative people in your life, and surround yourself with amazing winners instead. Imagine how much you could accomplish in just one year with a team of enthusiastic supporters cheering you on!

Don't settle for less. Don't allow people into your inner circle who drag you down or drain your energy. A lot of people don't know how to let people go, so they end up tolerating people they don't like or value. Successful people don't do that. They are always increasing their circle of influence, not saddling themselves with more dead weight.

When I'm coaching somebody new, I'm happy to give of my time, because my reward is seeing that person move up and succeed. However, if that person is not taking action but instead constantly making excuses or crying foul, I'm going to limit the amount of time I'm willing to spend with them.

If you're going to surround yourself with successful people, you'll have to eliminate those who seem to travel in a cloud of negative energy. Letting go of people is hard, but it's one of the best things you'll ever do.

So, how do you discern whom to eliminate from your life?

The people who are constantly giving excuses for their failures are never going to help you succeed. You know who those people are—you'll see their posts on Facebook, like a broken record. They're always a victim, they've always been hurt by somebody, and bad things are always happening to them. Most of these folks, in my experience, are attracting that negativity to themselves. A positive outlook begets more positivity, and vice versa.

When I took over F.I.R.E., there were only a handful of people actively doing firewalks. The unconstructive mind-set of company leadership had trickled down so that the most important element of the business—the firewalk—was suffering. Those few who did know how to create safe coal beds and be strong leaders had found out on their own. They were go-getters, but there weren't many of them. Now, rarely a day goes by that someone I trained is not doing a life-changing firewalk seminar somewhere in the world. I kept the successful people near me, which bred more success, and so on and so on in a positive cycle.

People flock toward like-minded people. This can work to your advantage or to your disadvantage. You have to start as you mean to go on, so don't invite any negative person into your life, or soon it will become a pity party.

Seek Out Positive People

Some might say you won't always know the difference between a glass-half-full optimist and an energy drain—until it's too late. I disagree. People will tell you who they are. You just have to listen. The founder of F.I.R.E. told me exactly who he was. I kept trying to do business with him for over a decade. He never failed to live up to the person he told me he was.

I have learned that there are three types of people in life.

The first type of person doesn't have any dreams or ambitions. They don't have goals and wouldn't know how to accomplish them if they did. I'll try to spend a little time with this type of person to help them develop their self-esteem and figure out their path in life. Often they just need to believe in themselves and their own abilities. But if they don't seem to get it after a while, I separate myself. Theirs is the kind of energy I don't need in my life.

The second type of person talks a good talk but never takes any action whatsoever. I know someone like this, a firewalk coach who became a good friend. He talked a good talk all the time, but he never seemed to follow through on anything. I never met a successful client of his. Many of the people he trained went bankrupt, which made me question his efficacy as an instructor. He spoke negatively about people who helped him and even about his own wife. He talked about how successful he was going to be, but I never saw it become reality. He talked the talk, but he didn't walk the walk.

The third type of person is the type I really like to surround myself with. These are the people who are goal oriented, who say what they mean and do what they say. They have things they want to accomplish in life. They may not be at the same point as me—they may even be far ahead of or behind where I am—but they want to go places, and I want to hang around people like that. These people look for reasons to succeed, and they don't stop until they reach their goals.

One of my mentors has about 220 fast-food chain stores and recently bragged good-naturedly to me that he did $7 million more in profit last year than the year before. Not too shabby, especially considering his total profit was near $50 million. Does this make me jealous of his success? No, it makes me competitive. It inspires me. I want that profit. It draws me to do more and be more.

Focus on what you want, not on what you don't want. (I'll talk more about this in Lesson No. 9 on knowing what you want.) Open your mind and heart to meeting positive people. Better yet, seek out those who match your values and fit into your intentional purpose.

One of my heroes in this department is John Brown. He runs the CEO Club of Dallas, and you will never hear him talk negatively about anybody. He doesn't allow himself to indulge in negativity. He purposefully avoids those people who are being negative.

Attracting positive people works in both directions: up and down. It applies not just to people you can train, but to mentors you can respect, admire, and follow. No matter where you are in business or in life, there's always someone to look up to. If you're in the mailroom, keep your eyes on that next level as you work your way up the ladder. If you're the CEO, perhaps it's another CEO, an industry leader, a respected national figure, or a higher power. Figure out who has something to teach you, and pursue that person's company and advice. Or get the help of a coach or mentor who has already been down the path and who can say, "Hey, stop looking at that seed you planted yesterday and congratulating yourself. We're on a five-year plan, and you still have four years and 364 days to go."

One of my core beliefs since starting my first businesses has been that I need to have mentors to guide me. Today, when people ask me some of the top reasons for my success, I tell them I learned at an early age that I don't know it all. I've always surrounded myself with people who know more than I do. It has come with a steep price tag at times, but I've always seen it as a good investment.

To get the right team in place, you have to have all the different working parts, not just people who are like you. Some people come up with the big picture. Others do the accounting and the business plans and make sure it all works. Having the right team includes having the rainmakers, the people in the field, those who make the relationships with customers and bring in the money. I've never done a business plan in my life, and I've had multiple million-dollar businesses. But I have other people who do those business plans and make sure it all comes out right. I have the right team in place, and that is a top priority to avoiding blind spots.

When you get the right people, they make an immediate impact. One in my organization now is Joe White. Joe took over the administration of F.I.R.E. and made an immediate impact. In fact, the sales were more than double the first year. Joe is a very success-ful coach and trainer, and he now works with my top FastBucks employees, producing amazing results.

Be open to learning, and welcome new people into your world who will elevate you. Knowledge is learned. Wisdom is earned.

I've often had great CFOs, attorneys, and sales-people on my staff before I could even hire them prop-erly. Instead I would give them stock to be part of the company, and in turn I got their expertise in areas I didn't have the time (or inclination) to really master.

It's easy to get into a blind spot when it comes to relationships, business or otherwise. Do you hire people or enter into business deals based on per-sonal relationships? That approach can cost you a great deal of heartache—not to mention money—and can cause your business to suffer. I have learned that making decisions based on personal feelings is often unwise. It is imperative to measure the employee's job performance by a standard that is both specific and consistent. People who seem like the best in the world can turn out to be dishonest or maybe just not right for the job or the company culture.

Make sure you're hanging out with the positive go-getters who have goals and dreams. In business, make your team a positive one. Hire people who take action and who will give you results because they are determined to succeed.

Stand on your principles as you do business and build your life. You have a choice: find out all the reasons to fail, or find out all the reasons to succeed. I want to dedicate my energy to people who find reasons to succeed. I want to eliminate the weak ones from my herd and surround myself with the strong ones.

What about you?

Personal Practice:
Surrounding Yourself with Success

Can you think of five positive, successful people in your life? What impact do they have?

Who could mentor you to a higher level? What sorts of skills and success would these people have?

Lesson No. 5

Stay Focused

"On my first firewalk, after I passed the halfway point," my friend and colleague Joe White has said, "I found myself thinking, *I am not feeling anything. I must have stepped off the coal bed.* So I made the biggest mistake in firewalking: I stopped. On the coals."

It must have been just for a second, but to Joe it felt like he stood there for minutes. He remembers that odd sensation when his feet informed his brain that his brain was wrong. He hadn't stepped off the bed—he was still on it!

The shock instantly snapped him back "in state." He said, "Cool moss, cool moss," over and over again, as fast as he could. He had learned to say this incantation as he walked on fire, and it has two purposes: First, it keeps your brain from telling you, "This is hot, this is hot." And second, it helps your brain focus on the image of a pleasant experience, an idea of walking calmly on cool moss or grass. Saying it enough times tricks your brain into focusing on something other than what you are actually doing—walking on twelve-hundred-degree coals.

Staying focused on a positive image helped Joe get to the other side of his very first coal bed, and it has helped him walk through fire ever since.

Keep on Walking

When faced with few good options, you can either stand still and do nothing, or walk across the hot coals of life. Go ahead and take the risk! The path that is easily traveled is rarely as rewarding as the one that has a few hot spots to navigate along the way. Focus on the end goal, not the difficult journey that will take you there. And no matter what, keep on walking.

My second big company, FastBucks, provides small, short-term loans to people who need money immediately but expect to pay it back soon. They find the convenience we offer worth the fee we charge— the annual percentage rate. But some members of the public and even some consumer groups are vocally against the product. They want to limit the fees we can charge, by instituting a 36 percent APR rate cap.

Banks aren't able to make loans of a few hundred dollars cost effectively, or they would be doing it. So instead they compete with our product by charging consumers NSF fees—penalties when their account has "nonsufficient funds." A customer who needs to borrow $100 for two weeks might pay a business like mine a $20 fee. The other option is to write three "hot checks" that end up costing the customer when they bounce: $75 or more if the bank clears the checks, or a whopping $150 or more if the bank returns the checks. If a 36 percent APR rate cap were in place, FastBucks would be permitted to charge the customer just $1.38.

I don't think many businesses would loan money to people with spotty credit (at best) for $1.38.

We provide a valuable, needed service at a modest profit. We have extremely happy customers. And we charge less than the major banks do. This has allowed the business to continue to succeed, and it's what I stay focused on.

Yet about ten years ago the New Mexico attorney general, unhappy that she could not convince legislators to eliminate the business, tried to institute a 36 percent APR rate cap herself. Many of my competitors gave up and went out of business. We initially felt defeated before we realized that creating such a law was not her job. We refocused our efforts and sued on behalf of the industry, and we got an injunction against the attorney general, prohibiting her from limiting APR rates.

Throughout this ordeal, I stayed focused and kept on walking.

Back in Lesson No. 1, I talked about the three main steps to success. The second step, ongoing willingness, is one that Joe White came to understand during his first forty-foot firewalk. The first fifteen feet were easy. Then, somewhere around twenty-five feet, he felt his mind drift. He was losing focus. Thoughts like, *God, this is long* and *Oh, that step was spicy!* and *When will I be at the end?* all rushed through his mind.

Most beginner and intermediate firewalks are eight to twelve feet long. A forty-footer is an advanced firewalk because it is much harder to stay in a peak emotional state. Staying focused for ten feet is very different from staying focused for forty feet. Being willing is easy in the beginning, but soon it becomes apparent that you need a little extra focus to maintain that willingness.

Seeking to complete a successful forty-foot firewalk is similar to having a long-term goal in business or in life. It is easy to be committed in the beginning, but to stay committed and stay on course, it is essential to stay focused for the long haul. Despite momentarily losing focus, Joe didn't sway from the task at hand. He stayed committed to and focused on his goal.

Willingness in firewalking is like life. You must be focused and stay focused to reach your goal. No matter what, you must keep on walking.

Eliminate Distractions

The nature of both firewalking and life is that when you set a goal, there are many things that will come and knock you off course or "out of state." As with choosing the people who will belong to our inner circle (which I discussed in Lesson No. 4), we may experience blind spots that detract from our focus on the end goal. Health, finances, and personal relationships are all potential distractions that prevent us from achieving our goals. It is difficult to manage our lives without dramatic shifts in focus among these crucial areas.

When we expend too much energy in one area, we tend to neglect another. In my life, for instance, I have been successful on the business end, but I've often neglected my health. I have found myself making poor food choices and not getting enough daily exercise. When I neglected my health, my energy levels were depleted. This impacted everything, including my blood sugar (I am a diabetic) and my mind-set. I could not perform at my best. The distraction of health issues—whether trying to take care of them or failing to do so—affected my ability to focus.

When distractions get us down, we often find ourselves faltering on our path. Negative thinking seeps in, and we begin to lose sight of the strides we are making. All throughout running my life and businesses, when this has happened to me, I've used three simple rules to get myself back on track and restore my focus:

Rule No. 1: See things how they are, not worse than they are.

Our natural response to negative situations is to go to the worst possible outcome. But that scary scenario is typically not likely to come true. Be honest with yourself, and allow yourself to see the true situation, not the worst-case scenario.

Rule No. 2: See things as you want them to be.

Envision yourself walking down the correct path toward your goals, free of distractions. Imagine yourself accomplishing those goals. There are a lot of distractions on the road to success. Don't get side-tracked. When you can see your path before you, it will be easier to follow it.

Rule No. 3: Make things as you want them to be.
Take your vision of your goals and make it your plan for reaching them. What's stopping you? Focus on doing everything you can to fulfill your ambitions.

As I will share with you in Lesson No. 11, businesses don't fail—people just give up. They lose focus, and then they lose hope. They start focusing on what they *don't* want instead of what they *do* want. Guess what happens to people who focus on what they don't want? That's exactly what they get. They can't strike a target they aren't focused on! So eventually they give up. From my perspective, however, giving up is the only true way to fail.

If you stay focused on your goals, there is always a way!

At my firewalk seminars, we also do an activity called a brick break, where I demonstrate how to break a real brick with your bare hand. One evening, my team was making the beds outside for a firewalk. We hadn't hired the fire department that night to oversee the fire, and I was starting to regret this decision. I grew anxious. I knew if the fire department saw our fire, they would put it out. My anxiety built up, and I knew I was losing my focus.

As I was preparing to demonstrate the brick break, all I could think about was whether the fire trucks were already on their way to put our fire out. I was focusing my energy on the phone. The phone *did* ring, and I did not pay attention to the brick as I was hitting it. So that brick became my blind spot—the distraction from my usual focus—and as I went to hit it, I broke my hand. That was a big lesson in losing focus on the present and falling prey to blind spots.

In both life and business, you'll need to confront a lot of firewalks and brick breaks. If you just freeze still on your path or drift away from your focus, you might get burned or otherwise suffer damage. If you keep on moving forward, though, the worst you will get is a little "kiss" (a blister). When you have to walk through fire, stay focused and keep on walking! Don't let anything distract you from achieving your dreams.

Personal Practice: Staying Focused

In what areas do you lack focus? What distractions are most difficult for you to overcome?

How can you practice improving your focus?

Choose Your Emotions

It was the first firewalk for Joe White, and he remembers looking for the coals. He could hear the banging of the tribal drums. It wasn't his turn yet, but he was in line. He was trying to peer around the people in front of him to see how long the line was, and to catch a glimpse of the coals that were said to be twelve hundred to eighteen hundred degrees in temperature. He would be walking over those coals shortly.

He was afraid but excited at the same time. *I have to see the coals*, he thought. *I have to see the coals.*

He was looking for certainty in an uncertain situation.

As the drums got louder, he remained focused on his goal. He could hear the people in front of him chanting, "Yes! Yes! Yes!" and then yelling and celebrating when someone reached the end of the coal bed.

Eventually he got close enough to see something glowing—the fire lane. It was mysterious and energizing at the same time.

Finally, he was next in line. His heart raced. Adrenaline filled his veins. He was ready. *You can do this*, he told himself, over and over. *This is your time to walk.* The moment had arrived, and there was nothing in front of him other than the fire lane.

Just as Joe was about to take that first step, he heard the word, "Refresh!"

Refresh? he thought. *What the heck is a refresh?*

Then he figured it out—they were adding new hot coals to the coal bed. The muted red-orange color of the coals that had been there were covered now by new coals that were a gleaming bright orange!

It knocked him "out of state." Suddenly his peace dissipated. He felt the uncertainty creep back in. He began to panic a little, until he heard a voice in his head. "Only you get to choose your emotions," it said.

I can choose fear or courage, thought Joe. He decided to choose courage.

So he made his power move, or "trigger," three times, shouting "Yes!" each time, as a way to anchor and recall positive emotions.

The guy responsible for assessing readiness at the front of the lane looked at him and said, "Walk!"

Joe walked. He felt strong and powerful, at the top of the world, full of courage and confidence. And even as he took step after step on the hot coals, he felt nothing else.

It was amazing.

Remember the Three-Day Rule

Choosing your emotions is more than just important—it is absolutely essential to your ability to react suitably and successfully to any event or in your life. Choosing your emotions is about self-awareness and being honest with yourself. How do you react to the world around you? Do you let your emotions rule, or do you take a step back and try to get perspective? Do you focus only on the tree directly in front of you, or can you see the forest through the trees?

You can't control everything that happens to you and your business, but you can control how you react to any situation. Putting your emotions aside and taking a calm approach can let you see the solutions to any obstacle.

First (as we discussed in Lesson No. 1), there must be awareness. You must be aware of where you are and what's going on around you. Only then can you take stock and see things for what they are, not just how you respond to them emotionally.

I did martial arts as a high school student in Austin, Texas. The school was Shaolin Martial Arts, founded by Grand Master Wonik Yi. Master Yi and the other instructors taught me so much about life while I was still at such an impressionable age. One of the many things I learned from Master Yi was this important saying:

> *Three times patience.*
> *Three times consider.*
> *Three times forgive.*

In other words, be aware of your mind-set and consider all of your actions. Taking a step back from your emotions isn't easy, but there is a simple way to do it: by using what I call the "three-day rule." Before making any major decision, consider it for three days. Don't do anything you might regret, simply because you're in a negative mood or you're angry or afraid about something. A decision made out of fear is never a good one.

I have used the three-day rule many times in my life. It helps avoid the confusing influence of emotions as you decide what practical action to take. It also teaches you to identify and understand your emotions, and over time you will develop the emotional maturity to make better decisions.

Emotional maturity makes one a much better manager. I found this out the hard way in my first real company, SmartCheck. I was young. I did not delegate. I had about 160 employees and a hierarchy of managers, but they had no authority. I micromanaged everything. At times, I let my temper get out of hand. This ran away many good employees.

Once, because of a cash-flow problem, we had to pay our clients late. My customer service manager came into my office one day nearly hysterical because she had had to listen to upset customers all day. I listened to her rant for five minutes or so, then tried to respond. I talked soft and low, hoping to calm her down. It didn't work. So finally, I shouted at the top of my voice, "Shut the f$#k up!"

She stared at me in silence for a few seconds, then said, "I quit." Then she walked out, never to be seen or heard from again. She had been a hard worker. It took three new employees to do her job, and none of them had the satisfaction rating she did. Had I realized back then the importance of controlling my temper—had I remembered to use the three-day rule—I wouldn't have lost a good employee.

We've all seen what happens when someone doesn't control their emotions. It leads to unnecessary conflict and fights, bad breakups, getting fired, and a whole host of other unpleasant situations. People who have no control over their emotions behave immaturely rather than responsibly. It's difficult to achieve success when you are not responsible for your actions.

I have learned many valuable lessons in business, but one of the most fundamental is: always keep your emotions in check.

Create Your Own Energy

Choosing and mastering your emotions isn't something you can just accomplish once and then check off your list. You have to work at it on a day-to-day basis. It does get easier, though, especially when you replace uncontrolled emotional responses with positive energy. At my company, we practice a daily chant, adapted from the mantra used by such successful entrepreneurs as Sam Walton, W. Clement Stone, and Napoleon Hill:

I feel great today!
I feel terrific!
I feel healthy!
I feel happy!
I have the power!
Yes! Yes! Yes!

I strongly recommend repeating a mantra like this—whether just for yourself or alongside your colleagues or employees—every day to help you create your own energy. You might want to change it around a little bit, like we did, but always say it in a loud, strong voice and use your body; make a power move. You can't be in a bad mood after you've said it. When I'm addressing difficult things within the company, or when there's an important meeting, we always do the chant first. It helps people get in a positive state, and then we move right into the problem at hand.

Saying a mantra isn't the only way to create your own positive energy. For example, music can have a powerful effect on your emotions, too. Think about it: If you're in a bad mood and you put on one of your favorite songs, you'll notice your mood changing right away.

One little trick I use to control my emotions is by organizing my music playlist into different categories. If I want to calm down and mellow out, I choose the playlist with calming, mellow music. If I want to get pumped up and powerful, like when I'm working out or about to go onstage, then I switch to that type of music. I use that music in my seminars, too, to get the crowd amped up and excited to learn and make a change in their lives.

You have to know yourself to really get your emotions under control. Be honest about what your triggers are. For example, at times my blood sugar goes ballistic and I don't think clearly. I become a crazy person, and when some little thing goes wrong, I think the end of the world is here. *My business is going bankrupt! Everyone is against me!* But I've gotten to know myself by now, and I know the drill. My self-awareness improves as time goes on. So once I realize that I'm feeling this way, I say my mantra to myself, start up the right playlist, and talk myself back to reality and rational thought: *Charles, five hours ago things were going just fine. This is all chemical. Wait until tomorrow, and your blood sugar will be back in line.* If I'm on the verge of making a big decision, I use the three-day rule. Then, once I get my clear head back, I press forward.

Remember, you can't control everything that happens to you and your business, but you can control how you react to each situation. With a little self-awareness and a few tricks up your sleeve, you can keep negative emotions in check and create your own positive energy. A calm, controlled approach can let you see the potential solutions to any obstacle in your path.

Personal Practice: Choose Your Emotions

What causes your emotional outbursts? Can you avoid the situations that trigger negative emotions?

How can you manage your emotions better? Imagine creating a playlist of mood music—what songs would be on your list?

Lesson No. 7

Be Yourself

I remember a lot of times in my life when people didn't like me. I spent so much time in high school and even during my first few years in business trying to figure out why. I knew I was doing the right things to stay on the path toward success. I knew I was being authentic, my true self. But it seemed there was always somebody who just had it in for me. Unfortunately, when you spend time trying to figure out why somebody doesn't love you, it drains your energy from what should be your true focus: your life and your business.

Being a teenager is a rough time. The chemicals in your brain are raging. In Lesson No. 6, I talked about managing your emotions—well, that's pretty hard to do when you're very young. I got really depressed at the age of thirteen and didn't know how to get out of that downward spiral. I felt as though no one loved me. I decided that life was just not worth living. My father was a pest control agent, and I had access to a chemical that's now banned, called chlordane. I drank plenty enough to kill myself.

Somehow, it did not kill me. I have the very distinct memory of being in the emergency room, watching over my body as the nurses and doctors pumped charcoal into my stomach to soak up the poison. I also have the memory of lying on a dry riverbed, and then going toward a bright light . . . only to have my deceased grandmother tell me, *It's too early. Go back.*

I went back.

I remained in the hospital for several days. At one point, I recall, an angel came to my hospital room with a message: I could not die until I fulfilled my purpose.

Until that point, I hadn't even known that I had a purpose.

I have never had the desire to take my own life again, nor do I get too hung up on whether people like me or not. Instead, I focus on staying true to myself. One of the things that I've learned throughout my life is that not everyone will like you. My advice: get over it. Just be yourself, and let the chips fall where they may.

Love Yourself First

The first rule of being yourself is to love yourself. As long as you know you're on the right path, don't worry about what other people think. Don't be a people pleaser. When people don't love you, keep on going. Not everyone will like you. So what? Deal with it. Move on. Be who you are. Love yourself.

This is a vital rule in life and in business. Many respected figures have failed or fallen victim to some sort of addiction because they wanted too much to be loved. The stress of wanting to be loved leads to a desire for more praise and applause. When it doesn't happen—when that absolute love doesn't come—people turn to something else to make them feel better or relieve the stress. They lose track of who they are and take desperate measures.

Many business leaders have failed because of greed, ego, and a desire for adoration. In other words, they cared too much what people think. When the focus is on what people think, it is difficult to be authentic.

Who are you?

Be you!

Determine your principles upfront, and envision the mission you have for yourself and your team. When you have established your values in advance, you will know when you're violating them because it will start to feel uncomfortable. Which values and principles resonate with you? Choose what you stand for, create your own platform, and implement your beliefs into your business.

As a public speaker I used to focus on the audience, with my eyes on every face, trying to develop a relationship with every single person out there. And I would look for people who didn't seem to be listening or getting the least bit out of it, and try to draw them in. I would focus on one or two people in the group at the expense of the rest of the group. Finally I realized I was doing it again—trying to get everyone to like me.

What I learned in time is that I was focusing on the wrong things. I was distracting myself by focusing on someone else's energy. This was hurting my speaking ability, and my presentations suffered. Now I get up on stage focused on myself and the message I have to share. I stand firm in the belief that I have a lesson to give. Even if only one person in the audience gets anything out of that lesson, then I have been successful and have done my job.

If you don't know who you are or what you believe in, no one will follow you. If you don't love yourself first, no one else will be able to love you. Be responsible for your own happiness. Find out your life's purpose, and act on it. If you don't know your life's purpose yet, you'd better work to figure it out. If there are bits you don't love about yourself, take action to change them—never forget that option is in your power. Head out for a long hike, go on a personal retreat, or take some time alone on a "date" with yourself. Discover your dream, and then do it. Discover your purpose here on earth, and then live it.

Don't Fuel the Fire

Having a compelling life purpose is one of the keys to being your most successful self. Being of service to others is another.

I have never had the desire to take my own life again. I've learned to manage my emotions (as I discussed in Lesson No. 6). And when I do get depressed, I get to work—on doing something for someone else. Some say that depression is a disease of selfishness: you cannot be working to help others and be depressed. For me, as for many people, I need only look to serve others, and that dark feeling goes away.

Another thing to keep in mind is not to let the turkeys get you down. I've had conflicts with people in business, but I haven't fueled the fire. I just don't add my energy to it, and it fizzles out.

As far as I'm concerned, it is a big world, and you have to maintain peace and live your life. Success without peace is not success, because you can't enjoy life if you're stressed out. Any lack of peace, no matter how slight, is too much.

One of my companies is in a controversial subprime loan industry. When I first started FastBucks, there was a lot of resistance to my business model. But it was worth persevering because years later, despite the naysayers, it is a company that I'm proud of. We have operations and managers in several different areas of the United States. We take care of our employees, and we've been very successful. People still say negative things about it sometimes, but I do it anyway. I believe that I'm helping people, a whole lot of people, and I believe it because I hear it from my own customers' mouths. Yes, if the product is used incorrectly, you can financially harm yourself. But we put in safeguards to keep people from doing so, especially over the long term. So I don't put fuel on that fire. I can't focus on the detractors or the negative people. I'm too busy focusing on my success.

Think about all the leaders and entrepreneurs and world changers who have had conflict in their life—people we pay attention to and remember, like Steve Jobs or Richard Branson. These are often the kind of people who shake things up and attract naysayers. But you can't be creative and different if you're always worrying about what other people think. Those people have all faced criticism, and it's possible you will, too. Learn to ignore the "Negative Nancys" and stay on your path.

Think about the president of our great country, who typically gives a powerful story at the State of the Union address, emphasizing how great the nation is from one side of the aisle—Democrat or Republican—and then, as expected, the other side tears into everything the president has said and makes it a negative. I always think how glad I am that I don't have to go through that—but we all have our own doubters and doomsayers to answer to.

At the same time, try to have some people on your team who aren't "yes" people. Some level of opposition within your team will cause you to think through everything you do and will make you a smarter person and businessperson. It's good to have honest people on your side to hold you accountable. But it's not good to have people who are continually haters, who are unnecessarily competitive with you, or who consistently refuse to support your ideas. Cultivate positive tension, not conflict. You want to encourage mutual respect and freedom to speak, but with the knowledge that positive action is the end goal.

When you reach a point where you realize someone does not have your back, try to move on as quickly as possible (as I talked about in Lesson No. 4). Don't add fuel to that fire. If you can't resolve the situation, find a way to leave it behind and just keep walking toward your goals and dreams.

At one of my speaking seminars, a former employee admitted on stage that she had left my company fifteen years previously to start a competing company. I was shocked! If I had known that at the time, it really would have bothered me. But I never found out about it, and by this time I had learned not to waste my energy on a negative response to this realization. It just didn't mean anything. Her company wasn't successful, but I was happy she took action on her dreams.

The point is, don't focus on what others do. Focus on your own success. It's like driving a race car around the track at the Indy 500: You can't keep looking at the guy behind you or beside you. You can't take your eye off the road and the sharp corners. You've got to accelerate and focus on winning the race.

What's your dream? Keep your eye on the ball. Don't worry about what others think or about the fires they try to start. Don't focus on getting people to love you. Not everyone will. Just be yourself. Be responsible for your own happiness.

Personal Practice: Being Yourself

What is your purpose? Do you remember to love yourself as you seek to fulfill that purpose?

What do you do when people don't like you or disagree with you? How can you change your negative reactions?

Overcome Adversity

One activity I teach in my seminars is the arrow break: You take an arrow and place the pointy end against the soft part of your throat. You take the other end and place it up against the wall. Then you thrust yourself forward.

If you do it rapidly and without hesitation, the arrow breaks and you feel little pain. However, as in life, hesitation can cause unnecessary pain. Failing to trust the process means the arrow won't break and you'll have to try and try again. Ouch!

The concept is often the same in business and life in general. Everyone encounters adversity and bumps in the road. The successful people plow right through it. Others hesitate to act, or they quit at the first sign of trouble rather than take steps to overcome it. I'm here to tell you that you can't be a successful entrepreneur without confronting a fair amount of challenges and jumping over plenty of obstacles. You simply have to get focused, get in your peak state, and believe it is possible to break that arrow.

See the Opportunity

Sometimes you'll face hard lessons in life that aren't necessarily related to other people, but are simply lessons that come from your own mistakes. These types of lessons can be a particularly hard pill to swallow. But who cares? Everyone makes mistakes! Don't dwell on yours, because that only makes it worse. Don't get stuck in a ditch; instead, keep your eye on what's on the other side. Whether the adversity or obstacle you face is self-imposed or external, focus on overcoming it.

The highest achievers in the world have overcome obstacles—sometimes enormous ones. The people who don't achieve their goals have come up against obstacles that they perceived as being bigger than they really were. So your dream just has to be bigger than any challenge you might face.

You see, every obstacle is actually an opportunity in disguise.

Take the story of my friend and fellow firewalk instructor, Brian Moore. After Brian had experienced a successful eighteen-year corporate career in the United Kingdom and Ireland, the universe provided him with an unforeseen opportunity. In 2003, Brian was a business director for Nortel Networks when the share price dropped overnight from $80 to $0.70. Devastating! Can you imagine losing all of that money and watching your career spiral down the drain before your eyes?

Yet this catastrophe was the catalyst that moved Brian to establish his company Peak Potential, dedicated to helping individuals and companies achieve more through mental toughness and resilience.

Brian has attained the highest-level qualifications in the science of achievement, quantum thinking, and neuroscience. He has studied and taught alongside the world's experts in personal development and success coaching—Tony Robbins, T. Harv Eker, Brian Tracy, and Jack Canfield, to name a few. In 2005, following a life-changing experience at a firewalk event in the United Kingdom, Brian decided to bring this experience to Ireland and beyond, by qualifying as a firewalk instructor. Thus, a failure in his corporate career led to the achievement of a lifelong dream.

Disappointments and disasters, misfortunes and fiascos—the most successful leaders consider it all learning and leadership preparation. They don't react with anger and bitterness after a mistake or even a tragedy. They don't get stuck in their emotions. They know there's no point in blowing a gasket anytime things don't go their way. When they do start to get stuck, they get out of it fast. Rather than wallow in emotions of the past, they take action in the present and find solutions for the future.

Look at any athlete who falls behind or sports team that's down in points. They don't give up. They push. They recommit themselves. They find a way around any obstacle. They dig deep and find a way to use their adversity to their advantage.

There is nothing like adversity to expose what is inside a person's heart.

Something as simple as a flat tire or an interview gone badly can offer opportunity for growth and learning. No one ever promised life would be a picnic. Without practice at failure and hardship, how can we develop the strength to handle our lives? Each experience, whether positive or negative, builds character. And the stronger your core character, the less likely you'll come undone at the first sign of difficulty. In fact, a bit of adversity in your life is more likely to prepare you to see when a great opportunity is staring you in the face.

Enjoy the Battle

How you manage stress matters—not just externally, in your speech and reactions, but within your body, too. And don't kid yourself: stress happens to everyone, and it will happen to you at some time or another. Being prepared for it can make all the difference.

So get ready for a tough fight, and try to enjoy the battle.

Adversity develops your principles. There are intangible qualities that you must demonstrate in order to succeed, and one of them is being prepared and willing to face adversity and thrive despite (or because of) it. When you expect trouble, you can learn to embrace it. There's no reason to panic over it. Be ready to greet it and overcome it.

I was raised in an abusive family. My stepfather regularly put my mother and me in the hospital. I remember one particular evening when my stepfather and my mother were breaking up. He was in a rage and had decided to take his half of everything—literally. He had a chainsaw out and was cutting everything in half. Huddled in fright on my bed, my stepbrother and I overheard him planning on taking his half of us. Knowing this life, I had stolen a gun. I had the gun in my hands now, pointed at the door. If he came through it, I was prepared to blow his head off. Luckily, he didn't.

Another time, he locked himself in the car in the garage with the exhaust pipe funneled through the window. Knowing we might not care if he took his own life, he made sure to keep our beloved dogs beside him, too. No, he wasn't exactly a great parent.

People use bad parents as an excuse for a life of crime or other failures. Instead, I used it as motivation to be independent, a survivor, and a success.

I was talking with an acquaintance recently, learning about her childhood, which was far worse than mine. At the age of five, with five sisters younger than ten, Lelani was left to fend for herself. Her mother was an alcoholic. There was rarely enough food. The family lived in a van and grew or found their own food. The kids learned to fish in the nearby river.

After listening to her story in near tears, I asked about her sisters. I already knew Lelani had a thriving business with multiple employees and two well-balanced kids attending college. I was happy to hear that all of her sisters turned out to be very successful, too. None of them used their difficult upbringing as an excuse to fail. Instead they stepped up and worked for the life they wanted.

Your past does not equal your future. Anyone can create the life of his or her dreams. Entrepreneur and motivational speaker Jim Rohn has explained that happiness and success are the result of how we live, not what we have. In other words, you can be as successful as you want to be, regardless of any adversity you might face. It's all in how you view the struggle and choose to fight the battles.

Take heart from these stories and others like them. Just as you can learn from your own experiences and struggles, you can learn from other people's experiences, too. Some of the most successful people in the world have rags-to-riches stories to tell, about facing hardship and tragedy, dealing with strained relationships, and repelling people who tried to hurt them or block their dreams. People who survive tough times are the ones who win.

I often think of my cousin and his amazing story. He's had it all: a mansion in North Dallas, a second home in Aspen, a private Gulfstream to fly him from place to place. His wife has a successful furniture store. At one time, one of his companies was building five hundred homes a year. And he's lost it all, too. However, he firmly believes that he can go from bankrupt to millionaire in a year or less. And as if to prove it, he has done so—five times. Think he enjoys the battle?

My personal belief is different: I will never go bankrupt, and I will earn more money year after year. Thus far I'm 100 percent successful in the former, and very successful in the latter. The key to my cousin's thinking, and the conviction that is paramount to my well-being, is that I know if I did lose it all, I would be OK. After all, I enjoy the battle, and I could do it all over again.

Many entrepreneurs risk everything, every day. If their business were to fail, they would be broke. They have grown aggressively, but they've put all their eggs in one basket. That's not my style. I subscribe to a disciplined approach to asset protection. I save aggressively for retirement, even though I don't expect I will ever retire. I invest in the stock market aggressively. I strive to have my living costs covered by at least three sources, two of which are passive. That means they continue to generate income for me even if I don't or can't actively work. Should adversity befall me, I will be prepared.

If necessary, I'll start the battle all over again.

Personal Practice: Overcoming Adversity

What do you do when things don't go your way?

How can you start to see the silver lining in any cloud?

Know What You Want

Firewalking has been practiced for thousands of years by people from all around the world. The earliest known reference to it is in a story from India, from about 1200 BC. Since then it has been observed as an organized event in many different cultures and religions, often as a rite of passage, a test of an individual's strength and courage, or a sign of one's faith. Like life, the experience can be both empowering and humbling. While there are various explanations, scientific and otherwise, as to how it is possible to walk across hot coals and not get burned, the fact is that only knowing what you believe and knowing what you want will get you safely to the other side.

The same is true for other exercises I teach, like the board break and the brick break. No matter your age, your shape, or your strength, even without any martial arts training, if you make a definite decision about what you want to accomplish and then give it everything you've got, you will break the board or brick. The reverse is also true: I have seen big, young, strong men come up to the board, not sure about what they want. And guess what? They don't break the board.

What do you want? Do you have specific goals to work toward? Or are you just aimlessly going through life, drifting from one venture to the next, never quite sure about your purpose? Successful entrepreneurs know what they want; even though they might not know at first how they're going to get it, they know they'll get it somehow.

Practice Intentionality

One of the things I've learned from guiding and coaching people throughout the years is that people who are unfocused do not get what they want. I talked a lot about this in Lesson No. 5—about how staying focused is crucial to success in anything. But what good is staying focused if you don't know what you should focus on?

We all know what happens when you've got a blind spot while you're driving down the highway. You try to switch lanes and almost sideswipe the car next to you. You didn't see it in your mirrors, because it was in that spot where your own car blocks you from see-ing the potential danger. The same thing happens in life, when your own issues keep you from seeing things clearly. Avoiding your blind spot is all about having a clear vision, and that means living with intentionality. If we don't have that clear vision of what we want to get out of life—if we have a blind spot—it really can lead to disaster.

The key is to be intentional—to keep your purpose in mind at all times as you take various actions. Living with intentionality is one of the traits of high achievers. Once I learned about intentionality, I started using it all the time. I realized that by knowing specifically what my goals are, I can achieve those goals and get whatever I want out of life and business. I could create my own reality (an idea I'll address further in Lesson No. 12).

In other words, practicing intentionality means you attract things to yourself according to the way you act, think, and intend. Whether it's health, wealth, or some other measure of success, be intentional about what you want, and you can achieve it. You build your own bridges, and it's your choice whether to build a bridge to success . . . or a bridge to nowhere.

Once, on a game drive in the African wilderness, I stated my intention to see rhinos. Within mere minutes, we saw two different sets of rhinoceroses. Later, as we made dinner plans, I said it was my intention to see a leopard at dinner. Ten minutes into our meal, a leopard approached the watering hole to drink. It may seem easy to dismiss this success as coincidence once in a day, but less so when it happens twice.

During my visit among the lions, I was told repeatedly the number one rule: do not run or fall. If you fall or run, the big cats' instincts will kick in. Getting into the enclosure with the younger cats, it's cute and funny when they try to trip you up. It's not so cute when they weigh several hundred pounds and are flying through the air at you, as was the case when we walked through the adult enclosure.

When the lion came at me, I grabbed ahold of his huge paws with the razor-sharp claws, or his gigantic head with the even sharper teeth bared at me. But I managed to act with intention. I did not run. I did not fall. Somewhere I found the courage and strength to shake that lion, throw him off me, and yell, "No! Bad lion!"

It worked. I knew what I wanted. The lion's intentions were not so clear—had he truly wanted to kill me, surely I would be dead. Had I stumbled and fallen, all nine big cats would have pounced on me instinctively and there would have been nothing to be done about it (gulp!).

Intentionality is key. Everything you do should be in line with your purpose.

Find Your Passion

As I said earlier, intentionality is a common trait among high achievers. One of my favorite high achievers is Napoleon Hill, who, in his book *Think and Grow Rich*, reveals the one thing you need in order to win: knowing what you want and possessing a burning desire to achieve it.

Take a journey within, and explore your self-awareness. Choose your goals carefully and intentionally. Make sure you have a burning desire to do whatever it is you're doing. Find out what excites you.

In everything that I do, I get myself worked up in excitement. I think about my goals and repeat them over and over to myself. I focus on the things that bring passion to my life and give me energy—the things that get me up early in the morning, giddy with excitement to move through the day. Those are the right things for me, the things that I make time to do in my life.

Find the right things for you, and make sure you're doing those things. Focus on the things that bring you closer to your goals, the things that make it difficult to settle down for sleep at night because you're so excited to get started on those goals. You'll know you've found your passion whenever you can't wait to see what the next day might bring.

Most people approach goal attainment by sticking just a toe into the water. But that's not really commitment, is it? When you find your passion, you don't want to dabble in it—you want to commit to it fully, with your whole heart and soul. I mentioned earlier that mere action is not enough; to be successful, you must take massive action. The same is true when it comes to your goals. Perhaps you have several passions, but to be successful, you must discover and pursue your burning desire in life.

You really need to know what you want in order to do that. If you set goals without that burning desire or that passion, you will likely not commit to getting them done. But if that which you pursue is big enough and important enough to you, then you will take massive action toward achieving it.

Here's an example:

Starting an exercise program is easy. Staying on an exercise program is difficult. Everyone wants to get fit, but no one wants to go to the gym. No one, that is, except the individual who is aware of and dedicated to the consistent action of working hard toward achieving their ultimate goal.

People become jazzed about starting. They buy the new sneakers, the cool workout gear, and the gym membership or the latest exercise DVD. Then, after the first or second week, the newness begins to wear off. They skip a workout, and then another. Next thing they know, the chair in the bedroom is wearing their favorite workout clothes more often than they are. What went wrong? Perhaps they weren't ready to commit, or they chose a method of exercise for which they just didn't feel that passion.

Let's paint a different scenario. What if the same people started off with some real soul searching, unearthed a true commitment to their burning desire, and then took massive action to achieve it? Sure, they went shopping for workout gear, but they also hired a personal trainer and did some research on eating healthy. Then they planned a month's worth of healthy meals and signed up for gym classes four days a week. They found a workout buddy, started a success journal, scheduled workouts on their calendar, and subscribed to a health and fitness magazine. They posted on Facebook about their goals and asked friends to support them. Now that's a commitment! These decisive actions provide a layer of accountability. It's not just a step toward the goal, but total immersion in that goal.

Which person do you think will be more successful over a period of time?

I've discovered that when people don't know what they want, they almost never can achieve it. They simply don't have the energy or focus for it, because they neglected to find their purpose and be intentional about achieving it. And sometimes people get so focused on monetizing their passion—on making money from it—that they are not focused on the burning desire that started it all. Don't let that be you. Find out what you want out of life, and live your passion.

Personal Practice: Knowing What You Want

What gets you out of bed in the morning, excited to start your day?

Once you've found your purpose, how can you remember to be intentional about achieving it?

Lesson No. 10

Focus on the Positive

One of the things we teach people in firewalking is that you absolutely must make up your mind ahead of time that you will succeed. You must cultivate a positive mind-set that allows you to see yourself successful and unharmed at the other end of the fire. If you're going into it halfway, with an attitude of *I can't do this* or *I'm afraid I'm going to fail*, I wouldn't want you even to try it yet. You're not ready to take action unless you are confident in your success, and for this you must be able to focus on the positive.

The first time I did the firewalk and succeeded, it felt amazing. What a breakthrough! I felt as though I could do anything. After that, it was easy. I continued to succeed. Eventually I realized that my fears had been self-imposed. I had created the limitations in my mind when instead I should have been creating positive energy. I transferred that life lesson to my business, and now I never forget that focus is a big part of success.

Think You Can

All the lessons in this book are closely entwined, because it takes each one of them to live your best life. I've talked about focusing on your convictions and believing in yourself to find out what is possible in life (Lesson No. 3). I've talked about focusing on people who succeed and who encourage you to succeed (Lesson No. 4). I've talked about staying focused on a positive image to get you to your end goal (Lesson No. 5). I've talked about focusing on staying true to yourself, not on what others think of you (Lesson No. 7). Well, each of these lessons is connected to the idea of focusing on the positive.

As Henry Ford, one of America's greatest entrepreneurs, wisely said, "Whether you think you can, or you think you can't—you're right." People believe they are not smart enough to start a business. They believe they don't have enough money. So those people don't start that business—and end up proving themselves right. But what if those people believed they were smart enough and could figure out a way regardless of their financial situation? They would start that business of their dreams—and prove themselves right, too.

Which type of person are you?

Some people simply believe they are not worthy of wealth, success, or happiness. A colleague whom I admired ran business networking groups with five thousand-plus members, and in fact was doing so well at getting people together that a gargantuan company like American Express supported her small business. She was great at bringing people together and connecting them, but her personal life was suffering.

Somewhere along the road she had picked up the self-limiting, negative belief system about money. She believed all people with money were greedy and self-centered, and she thought she could not have significant wealth and also have a relationship with God.

When she came to me for coaching, I was shocked. I tried to change her belief around, asking her to think about all the good she could do with significant wealth. What people could she help? What causes could she get involved in? It takes money to feed the hungry, to find disease cures, to educate and train people to better their lives. "Money does not make you evil," I said. "It gives you options!"

Here's what billionaire entrepreneur and business coach Dan Peña has to say about self-limiting beliefs:

> When your mom has Alzheimer's and your dad has emphysema, or your fourteen-year-old sister is pregnant with whomever, you need money to solve these problems . . . What money allows you to do, and what wealth creation allows you to do, is to have more choices in life. For those kids that wanna save the planet, they believe or worry about global warming, and they believe and worry about all these other things, the problems that we have in Europe. Go get rich and then take your money like Bill and Melinda Gates, Warren Buffett, and solve the problems. Don't just bitch about them!

I tell people, "Go out and be successful, and then you can use your success as an instrument to help others." I see too many of the kids don't do that. They think that carrying signs around parks is gonna save the world. Well, that's not gonna save the world! Let them go out and solve the problems of the world by creating wealth and then using that wealth to solve the problems.

Does your self-talk bring you down? Do you tell yourself all the things you can't do and rationalize why? Change that around. Focus on all the reasons you will accomplish your goals and dreams. You simply can't center your thinking on doubt and negativity, with questions like *Do I have the money? Do I have the talent? Will I fail?* You have to learn to trust yourself to do the things that need to be done.

Put in this light, it's clear that nothing is accomplished by focusing on the negative or expecting failure. Stay positive, and stay focused on success. When you think you can succeed, you will.

Be Open to Miracles

What thing have you been avoiding because you think you just can't succeed?

Back in Lesson No. 7, about the importance of just being yourself, I mentioned a time in my young life when I lost hope and ended up in the hospital after an attempted suicide. After what I'd done to my body, there was no way I should've been alive. Everybody said it was a miracle. What's more, I had the wonderful experience of sensing my grandmother's presence, even though she had been dead for some years, and of receiving a message from an angel. I'll never forget that experience as long as I live, and I'm grateful for my second chance. To me, this was the true—and truly unexpected—miracle.

Be open to the unexpected miracles in life. You'll get them!

Don't get me wrong—life is hard at times, and it's not always fair, either. (As you'll recall, I talked about overcoming adversity in Lesson No. 8.) People might do you wrong. Bad things happen to good people all the time. But are you going to close yourself off from success in an attempt to avoid failure? Are you going to wait for your turn for success, only to find that turn doesn't come to those who wait? Are you going to accept mediocrity or choose to settle for a life less than you really deserve? Or are you going to open yourself up to the possibilities and go for what you really want out of life?

I have come across many people who can't seem to escape the cycle of negativity—I call them "beaten dogs." They hate their job, or they hate being unemployed. They feel down and don't remember how to get back up. Their family and friends don't understand. Often they can't stop thinking about how they are just one among thousands of people seeking one of the very few good jobs available, and you can see the desperation in their eyes. Even their body language looks defeated. They've given up before they even start.

My advice to these people is to get into the practice of positivity. You have to open your mind up to the possible. You have to do whatever it takes—exercise, meditation, education, or whatever works for you personally—to help you focus on the positive. You need to be "in state" in everything you do.

Before giving a presentation, I get myself in that peak state. I explain to the audience that they, too, need to be in a peak state when searching for change in their career or their life. As you learned in Lesson No. 6 about choosing your emotions, I like to use a chant that goes like this:

> *I feel great today!*
> *I feel terrific!*
> *I feel healthy!*
> *I feel happy!*
> *I have the power!*
> *Yes! Yes! Yes!*

When chanted with energy and emotion and intention, these words fill you with a positive feeling about all the possibilities in your day.

Living, loving, stretching, and growing make life even more challenging, because you are living on point. But opening up to the miracles and daring to take chances has the potential to make life infinitely better, too. Don't let self-imposed fears and limitations stop you. Be intentional about focusing on the positive, and you'll overcome whatever obstacles appear in your path.

Remember, it's all in your mind! You have the power to be positive. Decide to be successful, and you will be. See your success, and it will happen.

Personal Practice: Focusing on the Positive

What self-imposed limitations would you like to let go of?

How do you get "in state"? What steps can you take to begin thinking you can?

Lesson No. 11

Never Give Up

Each firewalk is different, and each is a lesson waiting to be learned. As you wait your turn to walk, you clarify your intentions and focus on your goals. You dig into the inner strength you've built that allows you to overcome any challenge. You tap into the energy source you've developed within, and you walk.

After you reach the end of the fire lane and enjoy your moments of exultation, you review the experience and recognize that the air is clear of any fears or self-doubts. Your perspective has shifted: You see opportunities rather than obstacles—and see each obstacle as an opportunity. In your mind, remembered failures become lessons. It is perfectly clear that there's no reason ever to give up on your goals. As long as you don't give in, you will achieve them. It's only a matter of time.

Turn a Failure into a Lesson

My first acquisition ever was a company called Vali-Check. This company, created by former executives who had run the check verification and collection department for Southland, owner of the 7-Eleven stores, was a competitor of ours. At Southland, these guys were midlevel executives making midlevel executive pay, although I don't know the exact amount of pay. When they got Southland to let them take the business private, in their minds they needed to adjust their pay so it was commensurate with that of a business owner. So after opening their own business, each of them took a whopping salary.

When they came to me, they wanted to sell. They were losing hundreds of thousands of dollars. They wanted me to take over the business and assume about $100,000 worth of a business loan they had guaranteed. I looked at the business and saw that I had the capability to run it without them. I did the math: if I just eliminated their salaries, the business would make more than $1 million a year. I took the business off their hands.

If the owners had just taken another look at the business from an objective standpoint and reworked some of their salaries, they would've seen the potential. In time they could have grown the company to afford the salaries they wanted. The business was not failing; the owners had just given up.

I learned a lesson that day: Businesses don't fail. People give up. They just give up. About half of small businesses no longer exist within the first five years.[1] Why do you suppose that is? It's because people don't

1   U.S. Bureau of Labor Statistics, *Business Employment Dynamics,* May 7, 2014, http://www.bls.gov/bdm/entrepreneurship/bdm_chart3.htm

have the fortitude to keep going. When the going gets tough, they give up.

Think how successful you can be if you're someone who refuses to give up! Sure, you'll make a misstep in business here and there, and sometimes things can go terribly wrong. But if you're willing to learn from your mistakes and adjust your plan, then you can move on to the next, bigger, better success. In the long run, you'll never fail. You only fail when you stop, so keep going!

Seek out inspiration wherever it can be found. Surround yourself with successful people (as I discussed in Lesson No. 4), and let their determination guide you. Choose colleagues and friends who encourage you to keep on striving instead of throwing in the towel.

In my seminars, my job is to push people outside of their comfort zone. Sure, there will be failures. But we can turn each one into a lesson. I've made a commitment to myself: to keep coming up with new and creative ways to turn experiences into lifelong lessons. Sometimes they're lessons for my participants, and sometimes they become my own.

Push Yourself

I live in Hawaii part-time. I have always been attracted to the Big Island—it is small, country living, and the folks are just nice. I love the weather. I love the ocean. But what I'm really attracted to is the volcano.

A volcano is evidence of renewal. It's where new land is being created. It is a place that offers many powerful lessons—including one that really changed my life.

I took a group out to the volcano because I wanted to give participants the experience of walking on fresh lava. Sometimes you can drive right out to it. Other times you take a several-hour hike over old lava to get near the new stuff. This time, neither option was available. But I don't give up . . .

So we found a hiking company that takes you out in a van and guides you on private land through a rainforest, out to the active lava flow. They warned us that it would be extreme hiking. I told all my participants to expect it.

The walk out to the lava flow started at two o'clock in the afternoon. We reached our destination at six o'clock that evening—four hours just to hike three miles. At times we were in mud up to our hips. "Just hike," said the guides. "You'll get muddy, but just keep moving forward."

At first I wanted to avoid the mud, to walk around it. That desire went away soon, though—too much effort. At other times I felt completely stuck in the mud, like I would never move again. The guides kept moving, though, so we had to figure it out before they got too far away.

At last we reached the active flow. I felt such relief. We climbed up on it in the daylight and were quickly ushered about a quarter mile further in. The lava was overtaking the trees, and sometimes they became missiles. We had to be aware at all times.

We found a spot to sit down. The ground was hot, and nearby was a large opening where the lava flowed rapidly below. The guides wanted to show us flowing lava on the surface, at least a mile away. Some of us, however, were completely exhausted and decided to start the walk back instead.

We rested about half an hour. One guide had stayed with us, but she had never done the trip before. One of my participants was an experienced guide in Hawaii, though, and was confident he could find our way back.

It was nearly seven when we left. I was still so tired from the trip out that I was shaking. I slipped and fell several times, even on a flat surface. I began to rest more often—for about fifteen minutes, every fifteen minutes. *I'm not going to make it back,* I thought. *I just don't have it in me.* But what could I do? I was in the middle of a rainforest. No one could get me out. Only I could do that.

I had to push myself on.

Two hours into the return walk, we were overtaken by the other group that had hiked further on. As they passed, I felt what little energy I had left disappear from my body. But I didn't give up yet. Out of sheer competition, or perhaps it was simple fear of getting left behind, I kept moving. I did not take another break after that.

I pushed myself on.

Three hours later, at around midnight, I stopped responding to anyone who spoke to me. I had no food and no energy left. My blood sugar was as low as I'd ever felt it. The guide had been saying "Just ten minutes more" for the past two hours. If I'd had the energy in me, I would have killed him.

It was at this point that I came upon Cobus. Cobus is a hemophiliac. Because of this condition, his wrists and ankles don't work quite right. Yet I had seen him firewalk, walk on broken glass, and break boards and bricks—not once, but seven times each to become a F.I.R.E. Master Instructor—and now he had been walking for ten hours straight, through the rainforest and on a volcano.

Upon reaching Cobus, I went from holding a bitter silence to streaming a constant rush of tears. I'm reasonably healthy, and I had pushed my body far beyond what seemed possible. Imagine what he had been going through! I am so proud of Cobus—a true Superman. He pushed me out of my comfort zone and beyond the point at which I thought I had to give up. He reminded me that I had promised myself never to give up.

Somehow, I pushed on.

At one o'clock in the morning, eleven hours after starting that grueling walk, I finally got back to the van. I had been crying for an hour or more, and I had no tears left. My body was shaking badly. I was caked in mud from head to toe. I struggled to get my shoes off and discard them on the ground.

Sitting in the van waiting for others to arrive, I sat in silence amid the buzz of conversation, still not ready to respond to anyone. Finally, irritated by all the noise, I gathered the energy to utter my first words in several hours: "Shut. Up."

After ten minutes of silence, someone started laughing. It became contagious, and soon all of us were laughing. *Well, what do you know?* I thought. I hadn't given up after all.

The last participant got in the van at two o'clock in the morning. He was in the same mental and physical condition I had been suffering through an hour earlier. I said, "You may not believe it now, but soon you will laugh about this."

He just glared at me with eyes that could have killed.

Our entire group had pushed our bodies further than we ever thought we could do. Why? Because we had to. We literally had to succeed or die. When you make things a "must" in your life, you will absolutely accomplish them. We all made it, including Cobus. We never gave up, and to this day I am so proud of this group. We pushed ourselves further then we thought possible, and the strength we gained from the experience is priceless.

Don't allow yourself to give up on your goals and dreams. When you refuse to give up, you can do unimaginable things.

Personal Practice: Never Giving Up

What failures have you experienced? How can you turn them into lessons?

What could you do if you really pushed yourself?

Lesson No. 12

Create Your Own Reality

I talked in Lesson No. 5 about Joe White's first forty-footer. Well, it certainly wasn't his last. He recalls another forty-foot fire lane stretched out before him, but something was not right. The first few people who walked took only a few steps and then stepped off the lane.

Watching the group, Joe began to see the shift from certainty to uncertainty. People were looking around, shuffling their feet. The focus just wasn't there. The line started to stray, as people seemed to hesitate when walking up to the beginning of the lane for their turn. He could tell they were in their head, starting to believe it was too hot. Sure enough, the next person jumped off, and the person after that, too.

Then, as if by unspoken agreement, the next person waited while the group discussed theories about what was going on. Some people stated that the bed of coals was not ready for walking.

Then Joe stepped up to the lane.

He wanted to prove to them that the coals were ready, not as an act of bravado but simply to dispel these pervasive beliefs that had sprung up from the crowd. He made his power move and walked, calmly and evenly, with a smile on his face.

He made it across the coals. Those waiting to walk seemed to heave a collective sigh of relief and once again straightened into a confident line.

He had created his own reality.

Escape Groupthink

Joe's experience at that forty-footer is a perfect example of "groupthink," a phenomenon that is normal and evident in all aspects of life. But jumping into the thought pattern of the people around you is often a step in the wrong direction, toward self-deception and self-limitation. Will you listen to groupthink? Will you conform to the values and ideas of the crowd? Or will you refuse to accept self-limiting beliefs (as we learned in Lesson No. 10 about focusing on the positive), and instead set your own intentions (as we learned in Lesson No. 9 about knowing what you want)?

Joe refused to accept the crowd's limiting belief that the coals could not be crossed. He rejected the mob mentality and instead set his own intentions, acted on them successfully, and even made an impact on those around him.

Life is hard. It isn't always fair. These words are true, and yet these words do not change your ability to achieve your dream. Was that forty-foot firewalk hot?

Yes, but Joe refused to accept that reality. He refused to allow it to get in his way. He refused to be held back.

When you have failure in your mind, you fail even if you succeed. By focusing on the fear, you've already convinced yourself that you're going to fail. So when you finally set out to achieve your goal, no matter how large or small, somehow the residue of negativity—the little things you did not do right—stays in your mind regardless of your level of success. You end up wallowing in the failures instead of being able to celebrate the successes.

By creating your own reality, you are focusing on and celebrating success wherever you find it.

After my firewalk training, I immediately decided I wanted to be a F.I.R.E. Master Instructor. I wanted to have the best knowledge and be able to teach others. This set me on a course of many great lessons, perhaps the first of which was that I could decide my own fate, no matter how "outside the box" it might seem to others and even to myself.

On my last F.I.T. (Firewalk Instructor Training) course before becoming a Master Instructor, F.I.R.E. had a reunion event with all of the active master instructors. The founder and head of F.I.R.E. at the time introduced our final walk of the event by explaining that he wanted us to learn compassion for our future students. "My intention for this walk," he said, "is for everyone to get a burn."

At this time I had walked about two hundred times and had never received so much as a kiss. In fact,

I did not think it was possible for me to get burned. I had even started standing on the fire without getting burned. I believed I had "fire immunity."

So there I stood, watching everyone walk. And sure enough, in the same spot, everyone got a burn.

At first I just said to myself, *I'm not walking today. I don't want to get a burn.* Then I saw the founder looking at me. I imagined him thinking, *Charles is never going to be a Master Instructor if he doesn't walk today.* So I decided to walk. He did not care if I walked or not.

First I told myself I reject your reality that I'm going to get a burn. However I kept watching everyone get one. So I walked, and got my first and still only painful burn. I had fallen victim to groupthink.

After that walk, I sat with the other Master Instructors and began complaining about the pain in my foot. They ignored me. I complained louder. They still ignored me. But I wanted attention, darn it! So I complained as loudly as I could. Finally Gail Baiman, a quiet, demure, sweet lady, looked at me and said, "Charles, just say f$#k it."

That day, Gail and the fire taught me that what you don't put fuel on does not burn.

Set Your Intentions

It is amazing what we can achieve when we become resolute.

When that forty-foot firewalk seemed about to fall to pieces, Joe managed to escape groupthink and create his own reality because he was determined to succeed that day. He set his mind to it, and then he took massive and consistent action such that he could not have failed. He had so much momentum, and with each step he could feel himself growing stronger and stronger, that he walked straight into his own reality.

Setting my intentions and going after them like that is something that always has come natural to me as an entrepreneur. Some might call it simply "stubbornness," though of course this doesn't quite cover it. But even at my first firewalk, when I was petrified and couldn't bring myself to take that first step, I was determined to walk across those coals someday.

As I mentioned earlier, it was firewalk instructor John Maisel who got me across the coals the first time. He was also the one who introduced me to the power of setting intentions.

As the day of the course drew near, nervous and perhaps still looking for a way out of this first walk of my firewalk instructor training, I asked John, "What happens if it rains?" In fact, it had been raining for some time in Houston. I had joked that it was raining so much, all the animals were being loaded onto an ark.

"It won't," he replied with a smile. His reason? He and the others in charge had set their intentions. Their intentions did not include rain.

I rolled my eyes, of course, sure that this was no answer at all. I kept asking the same question, hoping to get a satisfactory answer. At last after several attempts, I finally got this answer: "If by some miracle it rains, I'll come back to do another walk—for no fee."

My friends and I mocked our instructor and his "setting intentions" for no rain all the way to where the course would be held in Houston. And indeed, it poured rain all day, each of the three days of my training.

Much to my surprise, however, each day when it came time to build the fire and walk, the rain would stop. Then it would start again after the firewalk was done. That's right—this happened three days in a row.

Though I still felt a little stubbornly resistant to this line of thinking, I started slowly opening my mind to the power of intention. Intentionality is part of getting to know yourself (as I discussed in Lesson No. 9) and learning to attract the positive to yourself. In other words, focusing on your purpose allows you to build the world you want to live in. Today when I do firewalks, like John, I set an intention of clear skies. Before I learned to set my intentions, there were times I canceled firewalks because of rain. Now that I believe in the power of intentions, I can't remember a firewalk I have canceled for rain.

You get what you focus on, so focus on strength. Most people do the opposite—they focus on avoiding the things they fear. But in business, you always have to show yourself in a positive mode. Fear is not an option. Turning back is not an option. Moving forward is the only way to go. So, find your passion and goals, set your intentions to achieve them, and stick to your guns. Seek out what brings you true happiness and joy, and include an intention for abundance in life.

As you create your reality, focus on what you want, not what you fear.

Personal Practice:
Creating Your Own Reality

What are some ways to avoid groupthink?

How can you set your own intentions?

Conquer Fear

A woman named Betty, who had joined Joe White's firewalking seminar, started her first day by walking through the door of the training center and asserting, "I am not going to walk, and don't even try to change my mind."

Yet that night, some sort of magic happened by the fire. Joe and his group were doing a forgiveness piece when Betty had an "aha!" moment. She realized that she had never forgiven her mom for leaving her and her dad, though she'd always thought that she had come to terms with that. As Betty watched the fire dance, she realized that up to that point, she had given only false forgiveness because she had been afraid.

She decided that she had to walk after all.

It was a beautiful, organic moment, a decision she made on her own, and an experience Joe will always remember. Betty told him afterward that what had thrust her beyond her fear was when he said to the group, "You cannot get where you want to be until you leave where you are." It was then she realized that the walk was about leaving the past behind for good and walking toward the woman, the mom, and the daughter that she wanted to be.

Later that evening, even before Joe had officially opened the firewalk, Betty ran up to the front of the lane and stood before the coal bed, with tears streaming down her face. "I need to go first," she said.

She crossed beautifully, and when she took her last step off the coal bed, the entire tribe shared in her joy, celebrating her breakthrough with hugs, laughter, and tears of joy, freedom, and release.

Walk Through It

Betty's walk is a classic example of the release from fear that can come with a significant experience or event in life, whether it's a physical test, a career milestone, or a personal achievement. Perhaps you see this event as an obstacle to be feared, or perhaps you are able to view it as an opportunity (as I discussed in Lesson No. 8 on overcoming adversity). But even opportunities can be frightening. Either way, it's a bump on your path, and you've got to get past it. Once you do, the way ahead will seem free and clear.

That has been a cornerstone of my personal philosophy for many years: identify what's holding you back, and move through it. It almost always boils down to fear on some level.

People ask me all the time, "Why do you firewalk?" To them, it seems there's not really any practical purpose for it. On the contrary, it does represent something very important: The walk represents the bumps we run into all our lives, whether in business or in our personal life. The walk is the fear that we create in our minds. We have to face these scary bumps in the road in order to move past them.

Mountain climbers facing a steep, snowy mountain don't focus on the fact that they might slip and die. That's just not what mountain climbers do. Instead they prepare themselves, set their intention to conquer the mountain, and take action.

If you want a great relationship but you've been burned before, it might be normal to have a little hesitation. But if you focus on the fear of getting into a relationship, you'll never have one.

Where's your focus? Are you going to focus on the fear, or on what you want?

We all have bumps that come up in our path, and they seem really big at the time. It's like the first time you walk on fire, you see this long, burning bed of red-hot coals, and it seems really insurmountable. But you get yourself "in state," you stay focused, you walk right across, you get to the end, you wipe your feet, and then you celebrate. You take each little bump one at a time. Then, for the rest of your life, that's a metaphor for you to remember: when you encounter the fires in life, you know that it's just another firewalk—you know to keep moving and you can conquer anything.

In life and in business, you run into plenty of bumps in the road, especially when you're starting a new endeavor. If you quit, it's just over. Remember (as I said in Lesson No. 11), businesses don't fail—people just give up. When bad things happen, you stay focused on the outcome, ignore all the distractions, and just keep going forward. When you face challenges or things that frighten you, just take a deep breath and go through them. You walk through your fear.

It's actually really easy to do (as you'll find out in Lesson No. 14), but we make things bigger in our mind and decide that they're difficult. We make mountains out of molehills, and it sabotages our success.

I am no different. The firewalk, for me, was terrifying at first. I went with the intention of walking. I went knowing that I would do it, and yet when I got out there and saw this big bonfire burning, suddenly all the reasons I was going to walk disappeared and were replaced by all the reasons I wasn't going to walk.

In life this can happen a thousand times, in a thousand situations. You get going in a business, but a challenge comes up—maybe a lawsuit, a new regulation, or a financial struggle. Or a new relationship is going strong in your life, until jealousy flares up or you have a disagreement of some kind. When this happens, you just need to focus on what you want, not what you fear. See things how you want them to be, and then walk through that fear and make things how you want them to be. Ignore the negative stuff. Ignore all of the excuses. Ignore all the reasons for fear and failure. Walk right through all that junk, keeping your thoughts only on the reasons for success.

Do Not Sit, Trip, or Fall

If there's one place you walk through where your fears would be justified, it's a cage full of lions. Yet here, of all places, is where focusing on your fear can be your downfall. So even in a lion cage you must conquer your fear and keep on walking. But whatever you do, don't run.

I learned so many lessons from that trip to play with lions! There are two rules when you are in the cage. Rule number one: never run. You act like prey if you run, and you can't outrun them anyway. Rule number two: stay standing. You want to be as big as possible. There's another way to state this rule, and it resonated so deeply that it has stuck with me, word for word, all these years: do not sit, trip, or fall.

Along with this, of course, is a similar lesson: don't hesitate. Hesitation causes pain. So you have to move decisively, yet without fumbling of stumbling—always moving, yet without running.

Seems like a tall order, doesn't it?

I went to Africa with the intention of getting in with the largest of the lions. I had done this at the Texas Exotic Feline Foundation. I felt that with the right attitude, I could do it in more wild conditions, too.

At this lion farm, as I mentioned earlier, the lions are kept together by age. After the six-month-old cubs (like the one that mauled my arm) come the twelve- to eighteen-month-olds—a whole lot bigger, weighing in at 150 pounds and more, eight to a cage.

The first day I went in, they were not so friendly, but I conquered my fear and entered the cage. I walked out without a scrape.

The next day was different, though, as I illustrated earlier in the book regarding my confrontation with the lions. Picking up on that story, we had been out running errands most of the day, and I had gone about ten hours without eating. Being a diabetic, I should eat small, frequent meals. So when I got in with the bigger lions, my blood sugar levels were off.

The lions must have sensed that something was off, because all eight of them came at me at once, from every direction.

Don't hesitate.

Don't stop moving.

Don't run.

Don't sit, trip, or fall.

I had to keep on going and forget about fear.

I kicked and hit at these wild beasts. The farm owner was kicking at them, too.

Out of the corner of my eye, I saw one young lion running and leaping though the air at me. I turned into him and grabbed his paws. What I didn't tell you earlier is that he tore my shirt, and suddenly I was bleeding. I held his paws, keeping his mouth away from my neck. And then I threw him down, pointed at him, and scolded him with my "No! Bad lion!"

It worked. We made our way out of the cage. But to later return to my room, we had to go *back through* the cage.

I never felt fear while all this was happening. After the ordeal, however, as the sun was setting, I realized that it was the time when wild animals go into hunting mode. Later that night, the owner told me that those young lions could have killed me. A lion's instincts are to take the weaker animals out of the equation, and a lion knows the weaker animal by its fear. The lions saw me as weak because of my health imbalance, but because I stood up to them with no fear, I am here to tell this story.

If I had allowed fear to unsettle me—if I had stumbled and fallen—there would have been nothing the owner could have done to save me. I had escaped a difficult situation without injury, because I had neither hurried nor hesitated to act. If only I could say the same for every difficult business situation I've ever encountered.

Personal Practice: Conquering Fear

What fears are the bumps in your path? What steps can you take to walk right through them?

What do you do when you are scared? Do you give in to that emotion, or do you stay focused and overcome it?

Lesson No. 14

Let It Be Easy

Even with my intent to walk, I had attempted a half dozen times unsuccessfully to firewalk at firewalking seminars. I had chickened out each time. I knew I wasn't going to give up, but somehow I just couldn't make it happen.

At these seminars, the instructor pairs you up with a partner. You then tell each other why you are going to firewalk. My partner went first. He told me that he had been burned over 50 percent of his body in a campfire accident many years earlier. He had been extremely afraid of fire ever since.

My partner's intent was to walk that night to get rid of the fear. As tears rolled down my face, he could tell I didn't understand. He was wearing pants and a long-sleeved shirt, so his burns were not visible. He showed me his burn scars. When my turn came, I told him, in tears, that I was there to support him.

I walked out to the fire with him. I watched him walk but I didn't follow, and I went to hide in the crowd ashamed.

After running away from the fire lane yet again, I finally hired a firewalk instructor to bring the walk to me instead. Everything was organized. The event would occur at my house. Surely this time I would be successful . . .

When I finally made it across for the first time, I cried for nearly five minutes. For years, I had made this so difficult in my own head, and suddenly I realized it was so easy. All I had to do was let it be easy, and it was.

See the Uncomplicated Route

Do you make life easy?

This is a universal lesson. Most of us tend to make things more difficult than necessary. We build things up to an unnecessary magnitude by thinking, rethinking, and rehashing every last moment in life. I do it, too—it seems to be human nature. Yet all aspects of life benefit when we stop making things so complicated. Our mental health, business, personal life, and relationships all suffer when we forget how easy the important things are—if only we let them be easy.

Business advisory group Forrester Research uses the mantra "effective, easy, and enjoyable" to describe the goal for any customer interaction. Letting it be easy is crucial, yet the concept really is as simple as that. All we have to do is get out of our head and get clear of the fear. Don't complicate things that are not complicated.

How many times do we focus on the struggle at hand—a difficult client, a costly mistake, a conflict with a loved one—instead of just letting it unfold, managing our stress, and waiting for it to smooth over? Next time, look for the uncomplicated route. It's as simple as flicking a light switch in your brain, reminding yourself that it's all in how you approach the situation. At my places of business, there are signs posted everywhere to remind people to let it be easy.

We all run into problems in life that we can't control. Maybe you have an important meeting or event to go to, and you get on the airplane only to find out that you are delayed on the runway. Worried that this delay might make you miss the meeting, you start to get angry. Your blood pressure is rising, your teeth are clenched, and you're getting all worked up. You're fidgeting in your seat and heaving frustrated sighs. Finally you exchange angry words with the flight attendants and, worst-case scenario, you get kicked off the plane.

Or . . . you could let it be easy. Kick back. Take off your shoes. Hey, there's nothing you can do about it anyway! So have a drink. Play a game or read a book. The flight will get there when it gets there. Let it be easy.

When I organize seminars, I often invite speakers to present on various topics. The majority of speakers make it easy. They get up, see the timer where it is supposed to be, and share their information. They do a great job onstage, and they let it be easy. They let it be fun, and it turns out great.

Human nature being what it is, however, some people complicate a simple matter and make things incredibly difficult. They have to hash out all the details down to the minute. What are the time limits? Where should they stand? Where will the chairs be placed? Will they have their own microphone? Then, once these answers are worked out, nothing can change. Most speakers have a great time, but these complicated speakers work themselves into a frenzy and make it a bad experience. Oftentimes, they selfishly dominate the promoter's time right before the event.

The fact is, things change. Projectors fail. Temperatures get hot. Microphones go out. Timelines are altered, and suddenly you are called on to talk more or less. That's life. It's messy. Professionals do the best they can with what they have. They expect the best, but are prepared for the worst.

It's up to us as individuals to make the choice in life to let it be easy. You always have the option to follow the path of least resistance in everything you do. That doesn't mean there won't be challenges— there will be, and there should be. Challenges help you grow and work toward greater success. But when you start to really complicate things, just remind yourself to let it be easy and make it fun. As I discussed in Lesson No. 6 about choosing your emotions, only you can control your response. Don't focus on the monsters under the bed. Are they really there, or did you create them?

Take It Easy on Yourself

I talked in the previous lesson about stepping over the bumps in your path and walking through your fear, and about how it's easy to do this when we recognize that we've made things out to be more difficult than they truly are. Even if you can't stop seeing those bumps as complicated, sometimes you've just got to fake it until you make it—tell yourself it's easy, and it will be. Tell yourself the fire is cool moss, and it will be.

Don't beat yourself up over this if you find that at first it's not as easy as it sounds. Old habits die hard, and you've probably always thought of your life as pretty complicated. But it doesn't have to be. Give yourself a break. Take time out for fun. Pat yourself on the back once in a while. Take it easy on yourself.

Like many entrepreneurs, I'm money motivated. I know money is not everything, and it doesn't automatically make you happy. Look at all the instant lottery winners and other millionaires who are less happy after winning or even earning all that money. I believe happiness comes from inside. But I also believe I can be happier when I have more choices—and money offers us choices. When my mom came to me a decade ago, broke and homeless, I would not have been able to help her if I were poor. Without money, I would not be able to support all the charities I do personally and through my companies.

I may be money motivated, but I also have a core belief in win-win situations. I believe we can all live a life of abundance. I believe in creating teams where we all win together. And I believe we can succeed in one area of life without sacrificing another.

Seeing people do more drives me to do and be more. This is something that people either get or really don't get. But sometimes you just have to set aside that inner drive, that tendency toward a Type A personality, and realize that you can achieve more by doing less. What's the point in working yourself to the bone if you never get to enjoy the fruits of your labor?

So, take it easy on yourself. Take a deep breath. Take a step back from the situation. Use the three-day rule I introduced in Lesson No. 6. With a little perspective (and a little practice), you'll see the benefits of just letting it be easy.

Yes, you should continue to drive hard, set high standards, and be relentless about accomplishing your goals. But you should also show yourself love and compassion. Life can be hard, especially when you are constantly challenging yourself. Being compassionate to yourself doesn't mean you are accepting mediocrity or choosing to settle for less than your dreams. It means you are smart enough to allow yourself to slow down, have a flexible attitude, and even make mistakes once in a while. Beating yourself up over it will only make things worse.

Life isn't always easy. If you approach it as though it is, however, it becomes easier.

Let it be easy.

Personal Practice: Letting It Be Easy

What have you overcomplicated in your life? What can you make easier?

How do you take care of yourself? How do you show yourself compassion?

Lesson No. 15

Pay Attention to Your Subconscious

During one of his early firewalks, when Joe stopped in the middle of the fire lane thinking he had stepped off the hot coal bed, a little voice inside his head must have said, *No, you're still on the coals. Get moving!* It was his subconscious, and when something like that happens for any of us, it's best to obey it.

If Joe had been more aware at the time, more in tune with his inner self, he would've heard that voice all along, telling him to keep on walking. If he had paid attention to his subconscious, I'm certain he never would have stopped.

Don't fall into the trap of taking one step forward, two steps back. We humans achieve through immersion, by being fully in the experience. The more we are immersed in a new experience, the more our subconscious accepts that experience as the new normal, and the more normal it seems, the longer we will happily remain there. But if we fall out of that realm, we subconsciously strive toward what was once familiar to us.

Your subconscious is a powerful internal resource. Try to be aware when it's at work. That way, you will learn when to listen to it and when to ignore it.

Cultivate Your Subconscious Mind

As long as you're alive, your mind is talking to you. It's always aware of something, and you inherently trust that awareness. When you are aligned with your core self, grounded in a state of certainty, that awareness acts as your inner guidance or intuition. When you are grounded in fear or uncertainty, however, your inner voice can start talking nonsense and lead you off your path to success.

The most powerful voice in the world is your own. Your subconscious mind is like a little genie in a bottle, offering to make your wishes come true. But sometimes that genie isn't very nice. It threatens to withhold your heart's desire. *You can't do it*, it says. *You're not good enough. You're not smart enough. You didn't come from a wealthy family. You'll never make it.* All that self-talk programs your subconscious mind with dangerous negativity.

The things we say to ourselves are just as important as what we say to other people. Toxic comments have to be weeded out and replaced with positive thoughts: *You can do it. The family you were born in doesn't matter. Adversity fuels your ambition and dreams. You are smart enough. You are good enough. In fact, you're great!* Then you must delete the negative comments you've made to yourself in the past—and don't let them creep back in! Once you uproot them, you'll be more aware of when negative self-talk or doubt shows up, because it will seem out of place.

Even the most successful people have doubts and fears running through their subconscious mind. But anyone can learn to rein in their negative mind and even harness the power of their subconscious.

As a successful entrepreneur I set goals, programming them into my subconscious, and even though I don't always know how I'm going to achieve them, I come up with all the actions. I trust myself to do the things that need to be done. I don't focus on negativity or allow doubts—*Do I have the money? Do I have the talent? Will I fail?*—to trouble my subconscious.

We all experience bumps in the road. At Smart-Check we lost our biggest client, Diamond Shamrock (now Valero), which had made up 60 percent of our business. I had guaranteed Diamond Shamrock's checks at a very low cost. The client was so big, and I charged so little, that once the client stopped paying us, I would not be able to stand behind those checks. In fact, on paper it appeared as though I owed Diamond Shamrock several million dollars, and I did not have the money.

Now, I don't read contracts. I trust my attorney with this aspect of the business. But in the middle of this situation, I awoke from a dream one night knowing something very specific about our contract with Diamond Shamrock. My subconscious had told me the checks were collateral. This meant I could send them back a pile of bad checks in lieu of several million dollars. I saved the company from failure and prevented a lawsuit. Furthermore, we replaced the client within sixty days and never laid off a single person.

Be careful what you tell your subconscious mind—and be careful to listen for what it's telling you. Although you're growing all the time on the subconscious level, sometimes you don't realize it until later. The conscious mind totally misses it. Then one day there comes an "aha!" moment when that information resurfaces, and you finally realize that something you learned in the past makes sense to you now. Every realization, like every experience, is a stepping-stone toward your future. Interpret it and ask your mind for more.

You know how the saying goes: "Be careful what you wish for, because you just might just get it." It also applies to what you think or say. So cultivate the garden of your mind. Imagine great things for yourself, and you just might get them!

Let Your Subconscious Be Your Guide . . . Usually

My first real company, SmartCheck, was my life for many years, and then I sold it. I was left with nothing more than a pile of money. Yes, I had all I'd asked for: I was a millionaire before age thirty. But I had nothing I really wanted.

I sank into depression trying to figure it out. What had gone wrong? I threw myself into that question, listened intently to my inner voice, and finally got my answer: *Selling your company wasn't really what you really wanted. It took your purpose away.*

So I started another business. Now I have multiple businesses, knowing that someday I can sell any of them if that's what I really want. This is the approach taken by a lot of successful people after they sell the initial business they had created as a labor of love. For an entrepreneur or any other type of creative person, immersing oneself in one's work is the only way to live.

Soon after that, I set a new goal: to be a billionaire by the time I am fifty. It's a long way from millionaire to billionaire, though, and time was ticking away in the back of my mind. So this time I had that self-talk in advance, and my inner voice said, *Well, maybe being a billionaire is not so important.* After all, I could live comfortably for the rest of my life with the millions I have. Did I really want to deal with that struggle?

Recently I started a new company, SecureVital. It is an online managed digital vault that keeps vital information safe, secure, and accessible when needed. SecureVital enables customers to manage their crucial information blocks in their lives—simply and securely. (Go to www.SecureVital.com for more information.) I set a goal for making that business worth over a billion dollars in a three-year period. Then I came to realize something very interesting: that three-year period of time would put me right at my fiftieth birthday. My subconscious mind had taken over and given me the ideas that would generate a billion-dollar company after all.

When you establish a goal, your subconscious mind goes to work. I had programmed my subconscious, and it kept on working toward that goal even when I tried to step back from it.

When I set goals now, I always add a caveat: ". . . or more." Sometimes we dream too small, and even our imagination can't imagine a dream so big. But our subconscious can.

One thing I want to stress here: money isn't everything. Some of the venture capitalists I'm working with look at my business and say, "Charles, I think if you go public, you can have a $10 billion potential valuation of your company." But from my perspective, if I take $1 billion off the table, instead I'll hit my goal of $1 billion liquidity and still own a good chunk of the company. And nothing excites me more than seeing people grow and hit their goals—not only me, but those around me. Money doesn't create happiness. For me, creating wealth through my businesses is about doing good things, and it's about helping other people do good things with their lives, too.

So this time, I'm listening to my subconscious.

In this next company, SecureVital, my goal is to help others hit their own goals. One way I do this now at FastBucks is by making all of my store managers owners of the business. And my subconscious is definitely cool with that. With SecureVital, I expect to make my initial investors and first employees very wealthy.

When you're in tune with your inner awareness, it will help guide you where you need to go, even if you're not sure how it's possible at the time. So no matter what you do, make sure you pay attention to what's in your subconscious mind. Sometimes it knows more than you do.

After I meet my billionaire goal, I look forward to implementing Bill and Melinda Gates's ideas of using a massive amount of their wealth to help the world.

Personal Practice:
Paying Attention to Your Subconscious

Does your subconscious mind speak kindly to you? If not, how can you start a positive inner dialogue?

Do you trust your subconscious to guide your actions? What did it say the last time you listened? What is it saying now?

Under-Promise and Over-Deliver

Throughout my career and my life, many people have told me what I could and could not do. They've told me to quit, said I was no good, or called me a failure. And each one of these doubts and insults only made me stronger and more sure of what I wanted. Their lack of belief in my potential made me work even harder.

For my friend and colleague Joe White, this all became crystal clear a few years back when he won an Entrepreneur of the Year award. In the history of this award, all the people who won had been bankers, CEOs of million-dollar companies, owners of restaurant chains . . . and now Joe, a recovering drug addict and alcoholic turned life coach and firewalk instructor.

After Joe gave his acceptance speech, as he was mingling with the guests, a gentleman he'd never met before approached him and introduced himself. This gentleman congratulated Joe and admitted he'd never heard of him before. Then he smiled, shook Joe's hand, and winked, saying, "I love hearing about an overnight success that took more than a decade to happen."

Even when you give it all you've got, some people will find you lacking. But that's nothing to worry about—it means there's nowhere to go but up.

Build Your Reputation

Practicing martial arts as a young man, I always wanted to spar with the very best black belts out there, even when I was only a white belt. Why? Because I wanted to learn. I knew I was on the bottom rung. Why would a black belt bother to spar with me? I'm sure it seemed as though I didn't have much to offer. But I wanted to deliver more than it seemed I could promise. They had nothing to prove, but I had everything to learn. How else was I going to become the best?

When you're filled with the drive to achieve, you give 110 percent no matter what—even if you're not sure your efforts will be valued or appreciated. Not only because this is the path to true happiness and fulfillment, but also because you never know who might be watching.

No matter what you do in life, you are going to need other people to help you do it. If you're starting a business, you will need other people's time and money. If you're working for someone, you will need to work hard so they remunerate you properly and help you move up the career ladder. Even if you were born with money or you won the lottery, you need to gain the respect of the people around you in order to be successful. The world works on relationships. And it's a small world!

At the age of eighteen, I served a short stint working for someone else. My job in the corporate office of World Cycle Corporation, a bicycle specialty retailer, wasn't big or important, but I gave it my best shot for as long as I was there. I'm sure management didn't expect too much out of a teenager, even if I had some experience running my own business already. But I was respectful, hardworking, and loyal. I tried to be innovative. When I left the company a year or so later, it was on good terms.

While at that company, I had started out in accounting. They had a manual system. I created spreadsheets to get the job done and get accurate numbers to management faster. The owner had gotten aggressive and raised a bunch of money too quickly. Soon the venture capitalists who invested the money put in a crisis management team. Most of senior management was let go; suddenly I was reporting to the crisis management team, traveling to all our stores, recruiting, hiring, and stabilizing morale.

Then, in my thirties, I needed a line of credit for my business. When I went in for a loan, I discovered that the loan officer's boss was none other than my boss at World Cycle. I barely had to fill out the paperwork—my old boss knew I was good for it. He saw that I had made something of myself and had something important to give back now, in the form of my own business. It was the fastest loan processing I've ever experienced.

Building and maintaining your reputation is extremely important, and this can be a precarious process. After all, it takes a lifetime to build and only moments to tear down. If you're honorable and you have a great reputation, people will remember you for that. There are many positive characteristics that can be part of a good reputation, but most of all it's really important to do what you say you're going to do. If possible, do a lot more.

At FastBucks one holiday season, some years ago, our projections said we needed $2 million for the holiday season. We had failed to apply for the credit line increase in time to get the money from our bank. We discussed the problem at our monthly management meeting, and everyone wracked their brain. Even though I typically pride myself on having the discipline not to take money out of the stock market for personal or business reasons, I was internally going through my stocks to figure out what I could sell to fund my company's needs.

It turned out I didn't have to. I was happy to get a call at last from one of my partners and long-term investors. "How much you need?" he asked.

I told him $2 million.

He asked how much I would pay in interest.

"How much do you want?" I asked

He told me, and I agreed. So he wired the money and then asked to have my attorney prepare the paperwork. The deal was done. And I would have starved before missing a payment to him.

Since then this same investor has come to the rescue many times over. He has even sent friends my way with large amounts to invest.

In 2013, the US government implemented Operation Choke Point, which impacted the short-term loan industry negatively. The purpose was to remove the industry's access to the banking system. All the major banks closed all of our bank accounts. At one time, FastBucks had an $8 million line of credit. Now, to my knowledge, no large banks will lend to any company in the industry. To get through the 2014 holiday season, FastBucks needed $1.5 million. I was able to completely secure those funds from friends and investors.

Without the trust I had built among them and all their colleagues, my business would have failed that year and many times over, before and since.

Refuse to Fail

In a book like this one about how to succeed, naturally the important topics include how not to fail. I've talked about not wallowing in the failures (Lesson No. 12: Create Your Own Reality), turning failures into valuable lessons (No. 11: Never Give Up), and overcoming your fear of failure (No. 13: Conquer Fear). For highly successful people, though, it all comes down to taking failure off the table altogether. Because to succeed, you must believe that failure is not an option.

Since banks will no longer extend FastBucks a line of credit, I have a pretty good excuse to fold the business—but I haven't. Instead, I've tried to remain calm but persistent. I refuse to give in. My happiness relies on knowing in my heart that I've made every effort to achieve my goals and take care of my people.

When you've got an "I can't fail" attitude, you'll do everything possible to make things work. One of the points I have learned to be very careful about, however, is the promises I make. I am even more careful about keeping those promises once made. I never promise more than I can deliver. Honesty is always the best policy. But you must be prepared to do whatever it takes to deliver on your promises, so beware of over-committing yourself—it could leave you scrambling to maintain your reputation.

Be persistent in keeping your promises, and others will know you for the trustworthy, sensible person you are. But what do you do when you make a promise it seems like you just can't keep? In the rare situation where you simply can't come through on a promise, work hard to overcome the failure and preserve your good name.

The reality is, no one wins all the time. Some entrepreneurs fail over and over again unapologetically. Whatever your politics, Donald Trump is one of those characters who has refused to take life lying down. He never seems to see his failures as failures. Even after a series of bankruptcies and failures, he has emerged from his financial failures as a credible media personality and businessman. His reputation is so strong with the American public that many called for him to run for president. Imagine that! If a businessman can fail, claim bankruptcy, and then go on to be respected enough to run for president of the country, just about anything is possible.

Deliver more than you promise, when at all possible. It's that kind of act that builds relationships and gains trust. Do not make failure an option. And if you do fail, bounce back. If you're giving anything less than your best, you're wasting everyone's time—especially your own.

Personal Practice:
Under-promising and Over-delivering

How do you build trust among your peers, colleagues, and loved ones?

Have you ever experienced a failure that damaged your reputation? How could you build it back up again?

Reward Loyalty

When I decided to buy F.I.R.E. from its founder, I worked with him over the course of a year on the transition. On top of the other doubts I had about his character, I soon found out that he had written a book about faking his own death when he was a young adult. He had watched his funeral and for some time had hidden the fact he was alive. In his book, he admitted that his parents had raised him well and that he just wanted attention. From what I could tell, he was still the same person today, aggressively trying to get attention—a loser in my book, not a winner.

I worked alongside his staff on numerous events as I decided whether to retain the current Master Instructors or develop my own. Having completed several acquisitions already, I knew that most businesses are their people. So of course, I wanted to work with people who knew the company intimately.

Until I got to know them better.

One Master Instructor from Sweden bragged that he had never honored his agreements with F.I.R.E. Another refused to do training events on his own but seemed perfectly content to ride someone else's coattails. It became obvious to me that the founder attracted people who were just like him. They were full of ego and lacked a positive attitude, a deep concern for the well-being of the business, and even basic loyalty to the company. Needless to say, I moved to develop my own team.

People quickly tell you who they are—you just have to listen. Like attracts like: Winners flock to winners. Losers flock to losers. So when you reward those you trust, and don't offer any incentive to the untrustworthy, you will soon gather a hardworking team willing to give you their time, energy, and best efforts.

Support the Trustworthy . . .

My job as a leader and an entrepreneur is to create a vision, inform a culture, and pull together the right team to work toward a common purpose. Beyond surrounding myself with good people (a concept introduced in Lesson No. 4), I need to do what it takes to keep those people ecstatic about their jobs.

Winners are hard to come by. If you have employees, partners, colleagues, or clients who are good to you, take good care of them, too. Reward their loyalty and build their trust, not just by compensating them appropriately (though you should do that, of course), but also through communication, conversation, and overcoming challenges together.

I love rewarding my employees. First of all, I create an environment in which people can thrive and be happy. We regularly schedule fun training events that people crave each year. We have contests that take people to all corners of the globe. Last year alone I led a trip to South Africa and another one to Thailand. I want people who work with me to succeed and to feel as if they're part of the family. I want them to have experiences that they will remember for a lifetime.

I reward those who work hard, and I encourage them to play hard, too. I have an oceanfront condo in Kailua-Kona, Hawaii, and I like to send people there. All my employees have free access to the condo anytime they want it. On their tenth anniversary with the company, employees get a paid trip for four to vacation there. My employees have full use of the condo, and they all seem to really enjoy it.

More important than trips and contests, I use words to make sure my people know how much they are appreciated. When you think of something kind and constructive to say, why keep it to yourself? When your people hear you affirming their efforts and value, it can go a long way toward building loyalty.

My entrepreneur ego sometimes gets in the way of this, because like a lot of entrepreneurs, I used to think I had to make all of the decisions. But now I see my employees as partners and I try to take the advice of one of my longtime mentors, businessman Jay Rodgers. Jay likes to work with people with great ideas. He invests in their companies, sells at the right time, and moves on. His advice: work yourself out of a job as quickly as you can. He's right. FastBucks runs just fine without me most of the time, and this allows me to follow my passion for teaching others and creating new businesses. When you have a company full of people whom you treat as partners rather than as the usual subordinates, you have loyal people who are dedicated to making the company better. It's not all on your back.

My head programmer, Chris Gamble, has had his hands on the FastBucks software for more than fifteen years now. He has always had my back, even when that has meant turning over work to others who were a better fit for my needs. Competitors and employees have come and gone, yet Chris has supported me through it all. Without his loyalty, more than once our software might have been tossed out—and the whole company along with it. When I started my new company, Secure-Vital, I made sure to get software bids because that's always the smart thing to do in business. But it was clear to me almost from the start that Chris would have the account, primarily because he earned my trust and loyalty a hundred times over while working with Fast-Bucks, and I know he will do a good job.

The rest of my IT team, Matt and Noah, have been with me from the beginning. We have never had downtime to speak of, and we have never had a data loss or breach. I regularly reward their loyalty, too, with fun meetings and events, great earnings, ownership potential, and trips to Hawaii and Thailand.

These are just a few examples from one corner of one of my companies. I also reward my investors' loyalty, most importantly with impeccable attention to keeping my word and creating a return on their investment. But I also say thank you by taking them on trips, buying them dinners, and just being there for them. I'm happy if I can be half the friend they have been to me. When I find trustworthy, dedicated investors, I strive to keep them for life, and I usually do.

I partially agreed with President Barack Obama when he said in 2012, "If you've got a business, you didn't build that. Somebody else made that happen." He was talking about the government that builds our roads and researches new technology and protects us, but it's also about the store-level employees and the entire management teams that go out there every day and build the small and large businesses in this country. If you don't reward those people, your business won't last very long.

. . . and Shed the Treacherous

A cab driver in Australia once said to me, "I love all my passengers—some of them while they are in my car, and some of them when they leave my car." Very funny, and a great way of looking at life: keep a positive attitude and learn from everyone.

I have learned great lessons in life from many different teachers. Some of them teach me the things to do, and from some I learn what not to do. I've had people betray me, and that was just as much a lesson as having loyal people support me.

For example, I employed someone whom I considered a friend, having ignored all the negatives so I could try to help him improve his career track record. This friend took over the management of F.I.R.E., but did nothing for our sales. So instead I hired him to coach my FastBucks company, yet he got no results. A few weeks and a $10,000 fee later, there was no real change. Still, I didn't fire him.

He quit.

In fact, this friend, to whom I had been loyal against all odds, wrote me a scathing letter, explaining that he was quitting F.I.R.E., and going to a competitor—the disagreeable man from whom I had bought F.I.R.E. several years earlier. Our sales contract had included a noncompete clause that had since expired, and the institute's founder had started a new business that was competing against mine.

After one event with the other company, my "friend" came back to me, saying unkind things about the other person and his training, and wanting to partner back up. What do you think my answer was?

No way.

I told this coach that he needed to be loyal to someone in his life, but he wasn't going to get that chance with me. I would never work with him again.

Often we want to give people a second chance, so we overlook things because we like them or want to remain close. And why not give people the benefit of the doubt? Some will let you down along the way, but you can't let it color the way you look at everyone else.

One disloyal human doesn't mean everyone else is the same. There are a lot of amazing people out there. Often I'll keep trying to help someone, even when I probably shouldn't—unless they totally breach the unspoken agreement about loyalty.

In most cases, it's best to let people go when you see the first sign they are not winners. Don't question your instinct, and don't waste time on people who aren't going to respond with loyalty. Move on without trying to revive a dead relationship or making an impossible personality fit in. Sometimes it's just not the right fit, and you do everyone a favor by letting the person move on.

Surround yourself with winners instead. Keep looking until you find them. When you find the right person, they will make an immediate impact. Joe White is one of those winners. I mentioned already that within one year of taking over the management of F.I.R.E., Joe had doubled our sales. This year that figure could quadruple. Support your winners, and be mindful of ways you can help them grow, and the benefits will go both ways. Having someone who fits in with your team or company culture is more important than having a high performer who lacks loyalty. Don't let one employee create continual conflict or drag down the morale of the team.

Good leaders develop people. They develop a positive culture and encourage teamwork. As Zig Ziglar said, "You don't build a business—you build people, and then people build the business." When you reward the positive, genuine people in your life, you will reap your own rewards.

Personal Practice: Rewarding Loyalty

What type of team are you building? Are you rewarding loyalty?

Do you give second chances too often? Not often enough?

Lesson No. 18

Envision the Outcome

Shortly after getting into firewalking, I held a charity event, trying to get some media attention. The firewalk was to support an individual who had been gravely injured in an accident and had no insurance. We let the press know that the event started at six o'clock that evening and ended at nine o'clock.

The television van and crew showed up at eight o'clock in the morning.

We had done nothing to set up, of course. No one else was due to arrive for ten hours. The TV personality was frantic. She had scheduled the whole day around the event, looking to do news cut-ins multiple times throughout the day. She and her entourage cussed us out and called us scam artists. It was very uncomfortable, to say the least.

I called my staff in early to help out. I reminded them to focus on the outcome. "It does not matter what she calls us or what she says to us," I told them. "What matters is that we get good press from this event."

So throughout the day, we did whatever she asked, even when she was asking us to do two things at once. We lit multiple fires for the TV cameras. We gave her a tour of the property. We brought the whole TV crew food for lunch and dinner. We handled a stressful situation with class.

By the end of the day, the TV reporter was happy—so happy that she asked about the other activities we taught. She gave us ideas to get more press. She gave me her card and said I should feel free to run ideas through her personally.

She got what she wanted. We got what we wanted. Why? Because we stayed focused on the desired outcome and discarded any words or actions that would distract from that outcome.

Don't Let Life Get in the Way

This is an excellent lesson in remaining calm despite what life throws at you. Many people have blown opportunities out of anger or pride. Who cares if you get a dose of a difficult reality or someone calls you names? Just move on and keep striving toward your goal. Remember Lesson No. 6—manage your emotions instead of letting them manage you. Take one step and then another. Don't let anything interrupt your pace. Step by step, keep on walking toward the outcome you desire.

Salespeople are taught that "no" just means "not right now" or "I don't know enough yet to buy." They learn that all the words and actions are just noise and mean nothing. A great salesperson will be subtly persistent until he or she answers all the objections and gets the sale. To be successful, a businessperson has to focus on the outcome and not get caught up in the whirlwind of details. It does not matter what people say or do along the way. What matters is the actual outcome.

The same thing happens in personal relationships: your partner or friend gets upset with you and calls you horrible names. Well, at least he or she is talking to you! Now you can address those concerns, listen, adapt, and converse. Manage the arrows as they are sent flying in your direction. Be calm and persistent, and keep working toward the peaceful resolution, the light at the end of the tunnel.

Earlier lessons touched on knowing what you want (No. 9) and seeing things as you want them to be (No. 5)—envisioning yourself walking down the path that is right for you until you reach your goal. This is advice that I have followed myself numerous times. In my business and personal life alike, I have faced situations that appeared to be bleak. But I learned to ignore the words and actions that did not create or support my outcome. Instead I focused only on the things that did support my outcome.

Lesson No. 10 pointed out that in firewalking, you must decide to be positive and know that you will succeed. To do this, you must see yourself successful and unharmed at the other end of the fire.

Even the world's top leaders face setbacks and must build resilience in order to overcome them. A lot of great men and women have overcome temporary snags and stumbling blocks by staying calm and holding out faith for the major rewards they knew would come later. Alan Mulally, Ford's incredibly successful and well-respected CEO for nearly a decade, was passed up for the CEO job at Boeing, where he had worked loyally for many years. But his attitude was to let it go. He took the setback in stride and was soon recruited for the top position at Ford.

One of the exercises in my goal-setting seminar involves working with the subconscious mind. I ask people to envision themselves having reached their goals. We want them to totally relax, but also to get really excited about finally achieving their dreams. We ask them to see themselves having accomplished their goal and even going beyond their goal. We ask them to see it happening more easily than they expected. We ask them to repeat it over and over to themselves: "I did it. I worked hard, and I finally did it." In order to imagine that and be convincing about it, you really need to know what you want. If you set a goal without that burning desire we talked about earlier, you're unlikely to commit to getting it done.

You can program your subconscious mind to focus on the outcome of success, and let your failures or setbacks roll off your back. Calmly creating that vision of the life you want can make all the difference in whether you fail or succeed.

See Beyond Your Goal

To walk across fire, or to smash your hand through a board or brick unharmed, it takes more than just seeing your goal—you must see beyond your goal. See your feet beyond the fire lane, or your hand beyond the board or brick. If your focus is on just wanting to hit the board or brick, your hand will stop there and you'll fail to reach your goal.

After reading *Think and Grow Rich* by Napoleon Hill as a young adult, I set two goals at the age of eighteen, as I mentioned earlier: to be a millionaire by age thirty and to be a billionaire by age fifty. I programmed these goals in my subconscious. I envisioned my first goal and then went beyond that goal. I'm still working on what comes next, but I know I won't stop at age fifty—or at a billion dollars.

My business is built exactly the way I programmed it in my head all those years ago.

My first employee at SmartCheck was a salesperson. He had recently retired from the military, so he already had an income from his pension. He just wanted something to do; he wanted to be a part of something. He worked on commission. Each day he would go out and sign up people for our service. He would come in at the end of the day with a stack of contracts and stacks of returned checks.

I developed a simple program to track both the customers and the checks. I entered the contracts and the returned checks, made collection calls, and sent letters while my partner made the sales calls.

The business grew from its own cash flow, and I changed my definition of millionaire by my thirtieth birthday, because my business was worth far more than a million dollars. Things were going great.

I grew SmartCheck until I was within six months of my thirtieth birthday. By then I had 160 employees and $20 million in revenue—but the most I had earned in this business was $60,000 a year.

I had failed to learn something: not to compete on price. I was being too competitive on price, so my profit margins were low. My business was definitely worth more than $1 million, but I did not feel like a millionaire. At this point I set a new goal: to be a liquid millionaire by age thirty.

I had six months to do it. I ended up selling the assets of my company, and I hit my goal of being a millionaire (many times over) just before my thirtieth birthday.

I used the same single-mindedness to obtain my ideal home. The house I live in now is the house I've always imagined myself living in. When I was about twenty years old, I would go on house tours while envisioning the perfect house for me. The house of my dreams was a good-sized house, set back off the street and with its own private body of water. That is exactly the house I got.

Time and time again I've seen people derailed by their setbacks because they wasted too much time on anger and bitterness. I've seen people limit their ambitions because they're afraid they're reaching too high. If you're doing any of that, you're not focused on abundance. Don't let any negatives derail the positive path you're on. Get focused on a successful outcome, and stay determined to get there.

Personal Practice: Envisioning the Outcome

Do you get caught up in the day-to-day details of life? Do anger, bitterness, anxiety, or fear hold you back from envisioning success?

How can you expand your goal horizon? What would happen if you stepped back for a new perspective?

Lesson No. 19

Step Forward

There's one last lesson you need to learn, and it's an important one. Luckily, it's an easy one because you don't have to think—you just have to do. It serves to tie all these lessons together nicely, with just one motion: step forward.

We don't always get what we want in life, but we will never get what we want in life if we never begin. You might have no desire to walk barefoot over a bed of burning hot coals. Believe me, originally I had no interest in doing so either! Regardless, there are things out there—your own personal fires—that you must cross to gain what you want out of life.

And every journey begins with a first step.

Accept the Pace of Change

Everyone goes through life at their own pace. No two steps are alike. Yet too often we become discouraged because we don't see change happening fast enough. We all, including me, love to see instant results, but that type of breakthrough or growth doesn't always happen. In fact, it is pretty rare.

In the realm of personal development and growth, the word "breakthrough" is often used. Perhaps it is overused. Too often we're taught to expect success to be an earth-shattering experience, as though the heavens will open up or you'll be hit by a bolt of lightning. Sure, there are many who experience success that way. But believe it or not, most of us don't.

There are really two types of breakthroughs. Some are evident immediately. We see and feel that change instantly. We have a new understanding, new knowledge. We see light where in the past we saw only darkness. Many of these breakthroughs will become integrated in our lives. Others, believe it or not, will dissipate as the euphoria subsides.

The other type of breakthrough is not as flashy, but it has staying power. It's an idea or innovation that becomes more and more evident as time goes by, until all of a sudden it shows up out of nowhere, and someone says, "Hey, I've noticed all the awesome changes you are making."

Perhaps the person who was stuck in fear now volunteers to lead a project, or the person who was never able to speak their own mind can now stand up in a situation when others may be critical. Perhaps it's the concept for a new business venture that you've been chewing on for many months or even years.

This is my favorite type of breakthrough, because though you really don't notice it, after it reveals itself you realize it's been there all along, building and building from that single first step you took, whether you knew it or not.

Never discount the power that comes from the momentum of action. We see it in professional sports when a team peaks at the right time—a team that began by seeming average can suddenly look and become unstoppable.

Another great example is the Chinese bamboo tree. You plant the seed and nothing happens. So you wait: Six months . . . nothing. One year . . . nothing. Two, three, four years . . . nothing. At what point do you say, "Hey, these seeds are bogus!" At what point do you give up? Well, the interesting thing about the Chinese bamboo tree is that it takes five years to germinate—but once it does, it will grow up to ninety feet in five weeks.

Amazing!

Life often mirrors the path of the Chinese bamboo tree. We think that just because we cannot see change, nothing is changing. Often that is not the truth. Sometimes great and marvelous things are happening while we are paying attention to something else.

There are plenty of ways to measure breakthroughs and results. Avoid getting locked into tunnel vision or comparing your path with someone else's. Take each step as it comes, at your own pace.

The rest of your life starts with every step.

Embrace the Opportunity

Earlier in this book, I talked about overcoming opportunity (Lesson No. 8) and never giving up (Lesson No. 11)—about seeing opportunities rather than obstacles. The secret is to embrace all chances, changes, breaks, openings, and prospects, because any one of these could be the opportunity you've been waiting for. All you can do is take it one step at a time and find out what's in store for you.

When I was too afraid to walk across the coals, I never would have guessed that a few years later, I would be at the Firewalking Institute of Research and Education, learning to be a firewalk instructor. Or that a few years later, I would move on to become a master firewalk instructor. Now I am one of the most active firewalk instructors in the world. And it all started with just one step forward. I saw an obstacle. Then I saw an opportunity. Then I embraced that opportunity.

That one hesitant, fear- and anxiety-filled walk was the start of a great journey and a new life.

It took me years to figure out all the lessons I learned that first night, and years after that to put them into words so I could share them with you. The funny thing about growing is that sometimes you grow and don't realize it until later. Growth happens on the subconscious level first and it happens all the time. One day we have an "aha!" moment when we finally realize something we learned in the past makes sense to us now.

In life, you will face disappointments. Step forward.

At times, you may think that everything is over and everything you have worked hard for all your life is gone, but step forward.

Friends and loved ones will betray your trust, but step forward.

Accidents beyond your control will happen, but step forward.

Just when you think everything is going perfect, surprise! You get fired or a key client leaves you. Dust it off and step forward.

Just like in the firewalk, just like in my lava trek to the top of a volcano, and just like in every other aspect of life—focus on that one next step, and step forward. Don't think too much about the second step, or the third, fourth, or fifth step. Don't think about how hard the journey will be. Focus on that one step.

And step forward.

Personal Practice: Stepping Forward

If the way to success is a unique path just for you, what might be your first step?

What might be your first step toward your ultimate goals and dreams?

Mastering the Lessons

I was on the other side of the coals now. I had completed my first firewalk. I remember looking back at them, disbelieving. I was amazed at what I had accomplished. I had been so scared . . . but I had faced my fears.

I was a badass firewalker.

Every experience is a stepping-stone toward the future. Every hot coal in life matters, providing you with the courage and fortitude and strength to achieve even more. Walking on fire—just like walking through the "fires" of life—gives you a sense of accomplishment so big, it makes you feel as if you can overcome anything.

And you can.

Firewalking gives us that amazing experience that transforms lives, and I have seen it time and time again. Like Betty, the woman who insisted she wasn't going to try it—and then passed a major milestone in her life. Like Brian, the executive who lost his job—and then started all over again, reaching even greater heights in his new life. Like Cobus, who pushed himself beyond all limits and never gave up. And like me.

In all things, I try to be the best I can be, and coaching is no different. But no matter how good a coach I am, the fire is always a better one. Through the thousands and thousands of individuals whom I have led across the coals, I am constantly reminded how powerful and omnipotent the fire is, and how the fire offers the perfect opportunity to gift each person with the lesson they need the most. Sometimes they are aware of what they need. Other times they think they know. And sometimes they think they need nothing—until the fire reveals the truth. No matter what they believe coming to the fire, what they receive at the fire is a life-changing breakthrough.

Most breakthroughs are like being in a dark room, unable to see or recognize anything (as I discussed in Lesson No. 19). Slowly, as our eyes adjust, we are able to make sense of our surroundings. There is a moment at last when we can see what before we were unable to see—yet this is not the breakthrough. It is merely a step in the breakthrough. It is only the first step, and that first step is awareness.

In Lesson No. 1, Take Action, I introduced three crucial steps to achieve success in any part of your life. Awareness is a great first step. Without awareness we see only what we have always seen, and we do only what we have always done, and in the end we get the same results we have always gotten. Awareness is essential for us to have a breakthrough, but it is a trap. It is too easy for us to think, once we've gained awareness, that because we know more, we have taken action.

But awareness in itself rarely produces enough action to create the desired result. Awareness too often breeds dabbling, that space where we take action at first, but once it becomes too challenging or the newness wears off, the action slowly disappears.

Awareness is essential, but so is the next step.

That step is willingness. Willingness is when we have an emotional stake, a true commitment. We have skin in the game. We care deeply about the outcome. Willingness is when we become ready to take action, to leave behind what is familiar and comfortable.

Awareness without willingness is like going up to the girl you had a crush on in grade school and asking, "If I asked you out for Friday, would you say yes?" There is no real commitment. If she says no, then your thirteen-year-old's rebuttal would be, "I was only playing."

Willingness is where it becomes real.

Yet as important as willingness is, it too is a trap! This time the trap is emotion, and the knowledge that what causes us to feel willing to take action today usually changes with time. For instance, if you have a business and your sales numbers are too low, the pain of where you are may create some willingness to take action. You might cold call to bring in new business. But once your numbers rise again, you may lose the desire that pushed you before. Pain can be a temporary motivator to succeed. For that motivation and success to be permanent, however, you must have ongoing willingness—willingness that evolves and morphs as you progress forward.

What drove me to do my first firewalk about ten years ago could never work for me today. It may be under the same banner, but it is a far cry from its infantile stages. Today I am motivated by other things. So willingness must be pliable. We must understand that it is too easy to get stuck in the rut of thinking, *Well, it has worked for me in the past, so it must work for me in the future.* Drive and motivation are functions of the now. Understanding and preparing for the rise and fall of willingness is essential to staying on track.

Once you have achieved awareness and can sustain ongoing willingness, then it is on to the third step: massive and consistent action. You simply must take action in order to live the life of your dreams. Awareness and willingness are critical, but I've seen plenty of people gain awareness of something they needed to do, and have the willingness to do it, without taking that next step toward action. It is not enough just to know what to do and to want to do it.

You must do it.

Not only that, but to achieve your goals and reach your desired outcome, you also need one final ingredient: consistency!

Consistency is the great equalizer when it comes to success. Talent, connections, being in the right place at the right time, and hard work are all powerful ingredients, but being consistent wins out almost all the time.

Sure, the first group may jump out in front—but those who stay the course and consistently continue to take action will always surpass those who were in front and do not.

Make your changes, and make your dreams a must. Commit to crossing the forty-foot firewalk in your life. Not to try it or to start it, but to do it.

Maybe it is part of my makeup, or maybe it's a remnant of my darker past, but I live by being all in or all out. When I am in, I am in. I live by taking massive and consistent action, and it has made all the difference.

I have never just dipped a toe into the water. I always dive in, though at times there was water awaiting me and at other times there was none to break my fall. But I always learned. I learned what not to do, I learned how to recover, and most important, I learned that no matter what happens or how bad it is, if I come out on the other side, I have won!

That has been a key learning in my life, especially in understanding about the breakthroughs that show up much later. I used to think that something was trying to get me, that things were happening to me. With years and experience come wisdom, however, and now I know that life, growth, and change happen all the time, whether I recognize it or not.

What's out there waiting for you? What breakthrough are you already in the midst of? Maybe it's not a firewalk, but I bet there's something out there that you must cross to have what you want. You may hear voices in your head saying you can't do it, or you're not good enough. Family and friends may tell you that you should not go after it. But the only voice you must listen to is the voice of your heart. If that voice says, "Walk!" then you must move forward—fully committed, aware, with ongoing willingness, and always taking massive and consistent action.

After reading this book and absorbing these lessons, I feel certain you can do it. But no matter what you're trying to achieve in life and business, it's your life and no one can take certain action but you.

All the magic happens after you take the first step. Step forward.

It is your turn to walk!

Acknowledgments

It takes many people to create a business, build a life, put forth a book. In my case, I am grateful to all those who taught me bits and pieces of the important lessons of life, which have come together over the years to create the book in your hands now. So if you worked for me or mentored me, or even if you somehow taught me what *not* to do, I thank you for your contribution.

There are two people, however, whose contributions have been absolutely essential to producing this book and to other elements of my business and my life: F.I.R.E.'s Dave Albin and Joe White. Their hard work, dedication, honesty, and loyalty shine through in everything they do, and I am eternally grateful for their thoughtful contributions to this book. People like Dave and Joe are the key to success in every sense of the word, and to them I'd like to offer my most heartfelt *thank you*.

Acknowledgments

Afterword

You have now read incredible stories of firewalking, of stepping into the unknown, of owning your power, and of breakthroughs. I trust you will use this book as a guide to inspire yourself to action. That action begins with the questions at the end of each chapter, but it does not end there. If you read this book and answer the questions, but then put it on a shelf to gather dust, the ultimate purpose of this book will have been missed. We are taught knowledge is power, but that is a lie. Knowledge is never power; it is only potential power. Knowledge is power when you apply it to action.

The lessons in these pages are here for you to take massive action to produce massive results! It's time to step outside your comfort zone and really discover your greatness. I must admit, I am a bit biased in favor of the life-changing programs we offer at the Firewalking Institute of Research and Education. When I travel and speak, I share my affinity for firewalking. People always come up to me to learn more, and my recommendation to them, and to you, always is to join us for one of our public firewalks. We have firewalk instructors all around the world. The transformation you experience from a firewalk is something you will embody for the rest of your life.

If you have a business, small or large, consider joining us for one of our firewalking team-building events. Corporate entities such as G.E., Google, Samsung, Whirlpool, Heineken, Reckitt Benckiser, and Kering all have used F.I.R.E. and firewalking to empower their people. Let us design a program for you. In addition to firewalking, we offer glass-walking, board and brick breaking, rebar bending, arrow snapping, and low ropes activities. I know it all can sound a little crazy, but as Steve Jobs said, "Here's to the crazy ones."

Perhaps you are a coach or trainer looking for new tools with which to create more change in your life as well as the lives of your clients. If that's the case, come and take part in our Firewalk Instructor Training. This training is conducted in more than five countries, where we teach you how to conduct safe and life-changing firewalking events.

To learn more about firewalking, corporate firewalks, and team building, or Firewalk Instructor Training, please visit www.Firewalking.com. Also note that Charles Horton, the incredibly successful business leader and author of this book, is available to speak to your company or organization. Please visit his website at www.CharlesHorton.com to learn more.

—Joe White
Firewalking Institute of Research and Education
(F.I.R.E.) Master Firewalking Instructor
Founder, Get Life Coaching

About the Author

Charles Horton is a successful entrepreneur with a passion for mentoring others. Founder and CEO of FastBucks, and founder of SecureVital, he began his journey by focusing on the things he found interesting: business, finance, and personal development. As a very young man, he created SmartCheck, a check guarantee company, and grew it to be the eighth-largest in the country.

An expert on personal finance, Charles has pursued business endeavors from an early age and has built several multi-million-dollar companies. He is also the CEO of the University of Wealth, which equips individuals and their families to create a legacy of financial strength and prosperity.

Charles is a F.I.R.E. Master Instructor and owner of the Firewalking Institute of Research and Education (F.I.R.E.), a transformative program for everyone involved. F.I.R.E. conducts training regularly for companies such as Google, General Electric, Whirlpool, Heineken, Reckitt Benckiser, and Kering. Charles also speaks internationally and is the author of several books, including the one you hold in your hands. If you would like to bring Charles to your company, visit www.Firewalking.com.

Charles is also an expert in developing corporate culture and crisis management. Visit his personal website at www.CharlesHorton.com.